China Shifts Gears

Urban and Industrial Environments
Series editor: Robert Gottlieb, Henry R. Luce Professor of Urban and Environmental Policy, Occidental College

For a complete list of books published in this series, please see the back of the book.

China Shifts Gears
Automakers, Oil, Pollution, and Development

Kelly Sims Gallagher

The MIT Press
Cambridge, Massachusetts
London, England

MIT Press books may be purchased at special quantity discounts for business or sales promotional use. For information, please e-mail special_sales@ mitpress.mit.edu or write to Special Sales Department, The MIT Press, 55 Hayward Street, Cambridge, MA 02142.

This book was set in Sabon by SNP Best-set Typesetter Ltd., Hong Kong and printed and bound in the United States of America. Printed on recycled paper.

Library of Congress Cataloging-in-Publication Data
Gallagher, Kelly Sims.
  China shifts gears : automakers, oil, pollution, and development / Kelly Sims Gallagher.
    p. cm.—(Urban and industrial environments)
  Includes bibliographical references and index.
  ISBN 0-262-07270-X (alk. paper)—ISBN 0-262-57232-X (pbk. : alk. paper)
  1. Automobile industry and trade—China. 2. Automobile industry and trade—Environmental aspects—China 3. Automobile industry and trade—Energy consumption—China I. Title. II. Series.
HD9710.C52G34   2006
338.4′76292220951—dc22
                                                            2005058373

10 9 8 7 6 5 4 3 2 1

Contents

Acknowledgments

I never knew the magnitude of the task before me when I set out to do this research. My thanks go to many people. I am indebted to Alice Amsden at MIT, William R. Moomaw and John Curtis Perry at The Fletcher School, and John P. Holdren at Harvard University. All are fabulous mentors, advisors, editors, and inspirations.

I am sure that this work would not have been possible without the selfless assistance of many people in China, especially Xu Jing, Zheng Fangneng, and Wang Lifang at the Ministry of Science and Technology (MOST), Zhang Jianwei, Zhang Jinhua, Wu Zhixin, and Wang Nan at the China Automotive Technology and Research Center (CATARC), Li Wenhua at the China Coal Research Institute, Wan Gang at Tongji University, and He Dongquan and others at the Energy Foundation in Beijing. Michael Walsh, Jonathan Sinton, and Feng An, all U.S.-based experts, were extremely helpful as well. I know I absorbed the valuable time of these individuals, and I will always be humbled by their efforts on my behalf. In addition, I wish to thank all of the people who took time from their busy schedules to share their wisdom in Beijing, Tianjin, Shanghai, Chongqing, Shantou, Ningbo, Detroit, Cambridge, and Washington, D.C.

Warm thanks to the members of the Energy Technology Innovation Project (ETIP) at the Belfer Center for Science & International Affairs (BCSIA) at the John F. Kennedy School of Government at Harvard University for their stimulating conversations, friendship, advice, and constructive comments. My colleague and sometimes research partner, Jimin Zhao (now at the University of Michigan), was a wonderful advisor in terms of research methods in the Chinese context, and I thank her for her generosity. Thanks go especially to Bob Frosch, Henry Lee, the late Vicki Norberg-Bohm, Hongyan He Oliver, Ambuj Sagar, and Guodong Sun for comments and constructive criticism. Professor Su Jun of Tsinghua University (and a former visiting scholar at BCSIA) not only had good insights about my research, but he was an entertaining language partner. Patricia McLaughlin and Dawn Hilali were excellent copyeditors and enduring sources of support. Any remaining errors are my own.

During the course of this research, ETIP received funding from the Energy Foundation, Heinz Family Foundation, William and Flora Hewlett Foundation, David and Lucile Packard Foundation, and Winslow Foundation, and all of these foundations supported this research in China. The Truman Foundation, Switzer Foundation, P.E.O Scholarship Fund, and The Fletcher School of Law & Diplomacy also provided support as well.

I also thank Clay Morgan and the others at The MIT Press who helped shepherd this book through its growing pains.

My parents, William J. Sims and Jo Ann Sims, encouraged me to find work that I believed in, and to endeavor to live a thoughtful and meaningful life. I thank them—along with my brother Colin Sims—for their constancy and love. My grandparents, Mildred Schooling and Ruth and Albert Sims, as well as aunts and uncles, were all exemplars, expressed boundless faith in me, and made critical contributions at times. One person deserves my deepest and most profound thanks: Kevin P. Gallagher. I am fortunate to have a husband who willingly engaged the intellectual dimensions of my work while providing much needed laughter, diversion, grounding, patience, and love. This book is dedicated to him.

1

Introduction

This book is about the rise of the automobile in China and the implications of China's growing automotive industry for oil consumption, emissions of conventional pollutants and greenhouse gases, and economic development. Determining how to contend with these competing pressures in China requires careful thought and attention. To resolve the seemingly incompatible goals of enhanced environmental protection, greater national security through fewer oil imports, and continued expansion of the manufacturing sector, China will be constantly "shifting gears" as it formulates new policies and economic-development strategies in the years ahead. The development and deployment of cleaner and more energy-efficient automotive technologies will be essential in order to reconcile the needs for environmental protection, national security, and economic growth in China.

The book investigates the extent to which technology transfer through foreign direct investment is an effective mechanism for the deployment of cleaner and more energy-efficient technologies in developing countries. In particular, the international technology transfer from U.S. automotive firms to their Chinese joint-venture partners from 1984 to 2002 is evaluated through empirical case studies. Of course much has occurred since 2002, and the book summarizes the major developments through mid-2005. There are three major Sino-U.S. joint ventures in the Chinese passenger-car industry. In chronological order, these are Beijing Jeep, Shanghai GM, and Chang'An Ford. All three are examined here.

A number of questions will be addressed in this book. First, to what extent did U.S. firms transfer their cleanest automotive technologies to China between 1984 and 2002? Second, to what extent has the transfer of automotive technology contributed to Chinese economic development, including the development of more advanced Chinese capabilities in automotive technology? Third, how have the automotive technologies that were transferred affected human health and environmental quality in China? Fourth, what factors on the U.S. side and on the Chinese side most influenced the patterns of transfer of automotive technology? Fifth, what can be gleaned from the answers to these questions about the incentives for and barriers to further automotive-technology transfer? Finally, based on the research, what can be inferred about China's ability to "leapfrog" to advanced technologies with the help of technology transfer?

Shifting Gears: Problems and Opportunities

The Chinese automobile industry, perhaps surprisingly, is still young. As late as 1990, only 42,000 cars were being produced each year in China, compared with 9 million in the United States. After the Cultural Revolution ended in the 1970s, Chinese firms lacked the technological capabilities to design and manufacture new cars, and so they turned to foreigners to acquire these advanced technologies, usually by forming joint ventures. The prospect of a thriving automobile industry in China was attractive to the Chinese government because such an industry could strongly contribute to economic development in China—and it was equally attractive to foreign investors because China appeared to be a new, untapped market with enormous potential for growth given China's huge population.

As of 1980, there were some benefits to the scarcity of passenger cars in China. Cars were not major sources of urban air pollution in China. Also, Chinese cars did not consume huge quantities of imported oil, as they did in the United States. During the twenty years between 1980 and 2000, motor vehicles emerged as a leading source of urban air pollution in China. Partly because of the growth in automobiles, Chinese demand for oil soared, ultimately causing China to become a net importer of oil by 1993, the world's fourth-largest importer as of 2004, and the second-largest consumer of oil in the world by 2005. The Chinese automobile industry took off economically, and in 2002, 1 million passenger cars were produced in China for the first time. China's automobile industry (including autos, motorcycles, engine, and parts-and-components industries) employed 1.6 million workers as of 2003 and accounted for about 6 percent of the total added value of manufacturing there that year (CATARC 2004a). The one constant in the midst of this massive change is that Chinese firms continue to be very dependent on their foreign partners for advanced technology.

There is an exceptional opportunity in China to shift gears and alter the trajectory of automobile growth by transferring cleaner technologies to China or by helping China cultivate its own manufacturing capabilities in clean automotive technologies. There are still relatively few passenger cars on the road in China—only about 16 million compared with 179 million in the United States as of 2004. Motor-vehicle oil consumption in China is currently one-tenth that of the United States, greenhouse-gas emissions from automobiles are still relatively modest, and the increasingly severe urban air pollution could be reversed through pollution-control measures.

During the 1990s, sales in new automobiles grew on average 27 percent annually, resulting in a doubling in the number of passenger vehicles on the road every two and a half years. The opportunity lies in taking advantage of such growth by installing, in every new car sold in China, the cleanest and most energy-efficient of the automotive technologies already sold commercially in the United States, Japan, and Europe. If this were done, urban air pollution could be minimized, a substantial part of the projected emissions of long-lived climate-altering greenhouse gases from the Chinese automobile sector could be averted, national oil imports could be contained, and the Chinese automobile industry could continue to flourish, contributing to China's steady economic development. Thus, this book aims to determine how the chances of this outcome could be increased based on an understanding of the historical record.

Terminology

A number of terms will be used throughout this study that should be clearly defined at the beginning. First and foremost, the term *automobiles* is defined to include passenger cars such as sedans and hatchbacks, and light trucks such as sport-utility vehicles (SUVs), pickup trucks, minibuses, and minivans. The term does not include large buses, heavy trucks, trains, or airplanes. Occasionally the term *motor vehicles* is used; this term does include buses and trucks. Light trucks are not commonly used as passenger cars in China, but increasingly, minivans and SUVs are being marketed to the Chinese consumer as passenger cars; two of the U.S. firms operating in China now produce SUVs.

It is also important to clarify what is meant by "cleaner" technology. An automobile can be made cleaner and more energy efficient through a combination of three measures: reducing tailpipe emissions of air pollutants, improving fuel efficiency, and using cleaner fuels. Tailpipe emissions of common air pollutants, including nitrogen oxides (NO_x), carbon monoxide (CO), and hydrocarbons (HC), are usually controlled through catalyst technology and onboard diagnostic (OBD) systems. Cleaner fuels—such as unleaded, low-sulfur, and compressed natural gas—can also contribute to reducing some of the harmful emissions of pollutants from an automobile. Emissions of the key greenhouse gas, carbon dioxide (CO_2), can be reduced to some extent from switching from petroleum-based fuels to alternative fuels, and net carbon emissions can also be reduced by using alcohol fuels derived from biomass (which removes carbon dioxide from the atmosphere when the crops are growing). Electric vehicles and vehicles powered by fuel cells operated on hydrogen are sometimes described as being completely clean, but their overall cleanliness depends on how the electricity or hydrogen is obtained. Today, hydrogen is usually produced from natural gas (with an associated release of the greenhouse gases to the atmosphere), and most electricity in China is generated by burning coal. In China, hydrogen would also probably be produced from coal. Of course, whatever the origin of the primary energy for vehicle propulsion, increasing the energy efficiency of the automobile can not only reduce oil consumption, but also reduce greenhouse gas emissions and the release of conventional pollutants as well.

Finally, the term *technology transfer* must be defined. Technology is understood to encompass both tangible goods or products, such as machinery, and tacit information, such as skills and knowledge (Grubler 1998). International technology transfer is thus the transfer of hardware, such as tooling for factories, and also the transfer of intangible assets such as product design and the capability of manufacturing a product. Brooks (1995, 83) argues that technology transfer is "a way of linking knowledge to need," and that it is a process of cumulative learning. This succinct definition illuminates several important characteristics of technology transfer. It affirms that technology should be conceived of as knowledge (Kranzberg 1986), and that technology transfer is a process of communication and education on the part of all parties involved. Martinot, Sinton, and Haddad (1997, 362) agree that "technology transfer is fundamentally a process of learning."

Methodology

Most of the empirical data were gathered through extensive interviews in the United States and China with government officials, firm representatives, and relevant experts. In total, from 1999 to 2003, ninety people were interviewed, occasionally multiple times. All but two of the interviews were conducted in person, and the exceptions were conducted by telephone. The majority of the interviews were conducted during the summer of 2002, at which time the relevant factories in China were visited. In China, interviews were conducted in Beijing, Tianjin, Shanghai, Chongqing, Ningbo, and Shantou. In the United States, interviews were conducted in Detroit, Ann Arbor, Cambridge, and Washington, D.C. As a rule, interviewees with Chinese citizenship are not identified by name to protect confidentiality, but the date and location of the interview and affiliation of the source are usually provided. Numerical data about the automobile industry in China were obtained from the China Automotive Technology and Research Center (CATARC) in Tianjin. Government documents, newspaper and magazine articles, and scholarly books and articles are also referenced.

This research is interdisciplinary in nature. Technology transfer from industrialized to developing countries can be analyzed from many disciplinary perspectives, including economics, political science, international relations, sociology, history, law, science, and engineering. For example, economics confirms that the acquisition of technology is necessary for economic development, and that there are many economic barriers to technology transfer. The political science discipline notes that institutions can strongly affect the nature and extent of technology transfer, and this discipline, among others, poses questions about the appropriateness and effectiveness of certain technologies for development. These questions posit whether the need for such technology creates a dependency on potentially domineering, richer countries, and whether such a dependency represents an unacceptable power imbalance between countries. Historians disentangle the causes of technology transfer and draw lessons from past experience that can be taken into consideration in the future. International relations theorists consider why there may be interests in technological cooperation or in withholding technology to balance power or to foster alliances. Lawyers formulate ways to facilitate technology transfer through international rules, private contracts, and domestic laws, for example, enhancing intellectual property rights or inhibiting transfer by erecting formidable legal barriers. There are also physical constraints that factor into the ability to transfer technologies, such as the quality of fuels available for use in automobiles. This book utilizes all of these disciplinary perspectives.

Road Map

The book begins with an exploration of the energy and environmental dimensions related to the rise of automobiles in China. The importance of the industry to economic and social development is discussed in chapter 3, as are the implications of China's entry into the World Trade Organization (WTO) for this sector. Chapter 4 traces the history of foreign technology in the Chinese automobile industry and the role of the Chinese government in helping the sector to develop. The three main case studies of Beijing Jeep, Shanghai GM, and Chang'An Ford are explored in detail in the following three chapters. Then, the energy and environmental implications of technology transfer in the automobile industry are evaluated in chapter 8, and the impact of technology transfer on the economic development of the industry is assessed in chapter 9. Finally, policy recommendations for the Chinese and U.S. governments are set forth at the end of the book.

2

The Energy and Environmental Dimensions of Cars in China

Ask almost any urban Chinese citizen if he or she would like to own a car, and you will usually get an affirmative answer. In the last decade, the prospect of attracting millions of Chinese car buyers has propelled both foreign and domestic auto manufacturers to pour billions of dollars into developing a vibrant automobile industry in China. Yet, as automobile production surged upward during the 1990s, questions started to arise, both within China and internationally, about the implications of such explosive growth in the Chinese automobile industry (World Bank 1997; Shao and Zhang 2001; EIA 2001). In particular, the connections and trade-offs among economic development, energy use, and environmental quality began to be discussed. This chapter will explore the energy and environmental dimensions of motorization in China.

Although few Chinese can actually afford to purchase a car now, the potential exists for substantial demand for automobiles in the near future. Indeed, the growth in passenger-car production was explosive from 2000 to 2005, as can be seen in figure 2.1.

As of the end of 2004, there were 16 million passenger cars (cars, minivans, SUVs) on the road in China. There were also 60 million motorcycles, 8 million large buses, and 8.5 million trucks as of 2003 (CATARC 2004a).

Having all these new vehicles on the road has transformed Chinese city streets from being clogged with bicycles into being jammed with cars, buses, and motorcycles (although the latter have been banned in several large cities). The SARS outbreak contributed to the sharp rise in private ownership of vehicles because people wanted to be isolated from their fellow commuters. People also now feel they are taking their life into

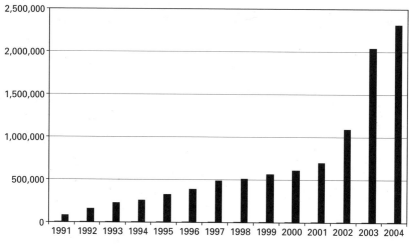

Figure 2.1
Passenger-car production in China (1991–2004) (*data sources*: CATARC 2004a; CATARC 2005)

their hands if they travel by bicycle due to the chaos and congestion on the streets. In rural areas, private ownership of cars is still very low. There were an estimated 22 million three- and four-wheel rural vehicles in China as of 2001, most of which used small, diesel-powered engines. These vehicles are primarily used to transport goods, and transporting people is a secondary use (Sperling, Lin, and Hamilton 2004).

Today, with 20 percent of the world's population, Chinese citizens still own just 1.5 percent of the total number of cars in the world. This is in stark contrast to the situation in the United States, where with only 5 percent of the world's population, U.S. citizens own 25 percent of the world's cars. In other words, China currently has about the same number of cars per person as the United States did in 1913 (Davis and Diegel 2002).

Energy Dimensions of Automobiles in China

Passenger cars do not currently consume very much energy in China because there are still relatively few cars on the road; most of the related energy concerns arise when one thinks of future automotive oil

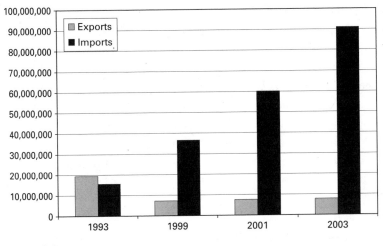

Figure 2.2
Chinese crude imports and exports (*data sources*: LBNL 2001; BP 2004)

consumption. As of 2002, the entire transportation sector only consumed 7 percent of the commercial energy supply (EIA 2002). In 2003, motor vehicles consumed 1.2 million barrels per day, about one-third of total Chinese crude-oil production (CATARC 2004a; EIA 2002).[1]

Any visitor to one of China's big cities cannot help but notice that these cities are already jammed with automobiles. Most of China's 16 million passenger cars are used in cities. In fact, 17 percent of all of China's cars are located in just four cities: Beijing, Shanghai, Chongqing, and Tianjin (CATARC 2004a). These urbanites are not just puttering around the city; they also seem to enjoy hitting the open road. Beijing alone reportedly has thirty automobile clubs, including one called the "Off Roader 4WD Club" (Liu 2002), where people gather to drive their rugged vehicles long distances over the countryside. Rising oil consumption emerged as a major concern when China became a net oil importer after 1993, as shown in figure 2.2. China only holds 2 percent of world oil reserves (BP 2004), so traditionally oil was mainly used in industrial boilers. Partly because of the rising popularity of automobiles, both oil consumption and oil imports grew rapidly during the 1990s. By 2000, total Chinese automobile oil consumption equaled total oil imports at about 1.2 million barrels per day (Xu 2002).

As of 2004, imports had risen to 2.4 million barrels per day (compared with 10 million barrels per day for the United States), making China the fourth-largest oil importer in the world after the United States, Europe, and Japan. China already imports a greater percentage of its oil from the Middle East than the United States does. More than half of China's current oil imports come from the Persian Gulf region, compared with just one-quarter of U.S. imports. Given its increasing dependence on the Middle East, China has predictably signed major oil exploration and production contracts worth billions of dollars during the past ten years with a number of foreign countries—including Peru, Sudan, Iraq, Venezuela, and Kazakhstan—to guarantee its oil supplies into the future (X. Xu 2000).

In this chapter a number of scenarios about future automotive oil consumption are explored in order to provide a general range of estimates about Chinese passenger-car oil consumption in 2020. These scenarios are based on three simple variables: the number of people who will purchase cars, the fuel efficiency of the automobiles purchased, and the number of miles the cars are driven each year. Table 2.1 offers a presentation of these scenarios and depicts how those three variables can interact with each other. The scenarios can be grouped into three main categories:

Best-Case Scenarios

China's automotive oil consumption in 2020 could be less than 1 million barrels per day if

• China's annual growth in automobile sales is considerably slower than it was on average during the 1990s (18 percent on average), perhaps because good public transportation alternatives are provided; and
• Chinese fuel efficiency doubles from 2002-average U.S. fuel economy to 50 mpg by 2020 (the level of commercially available hybrid-electric cars); and
• Chinese drivers drive only 5,000 miles each year, significantly less than their Japanese counterparts, who drive 7,500 miles a year.

Midrange Scenarios

China's automotive oil consumption could be 1–5 million barrels per day in 2020 if

Table 2.1
Scenarios for Chinese automotive oil consumption in 2020

Assumption	Number of cars (million)	Average fuel economy (mpg)	Miles driven per year	Oil consumption (M bbls/day)
Low growth, high efficiency, low miles	45	50	5,000	0.3
Low growth, medium efficiency, medium miles	45	35	7,500	0.6
Low growth, low efficiency, medium miles	45	24	7,500	0.9
Medium growth, high efficiency, low miles	110	50	5,000	0.7
Medium growth, medium efficiency, medium miles	110	35	7,500	1.5
Medium growth, low efficiency, low miles	110	24	5,000	1.5
Medium growth, low efficiency, medium miles	110	24	7,500	2.2
Medium growth, low efficiency, high miles	110	24	11,000	3.3
High growth, high efficiency, low miles	245	50	5,000	1.6
High growth, medium efficiency, medium miles	245	35	7,500	3.4
High growth, low efficiency, medium miles	245	24	7,500	5.0
Very high growth, high efficiency, low miles	830	50	5,000	5.4
Very high growth, medium efficiency, medium miles	830	35	7,500	11.6
Very high growth, low efficiency, high miles	830	24	11,000	24.8

Notes:
Low growth: (10% annually) is slower growth in the number of passenger cars sold annually in China than the actual average 1990s growth, which was 18%.
Medium growth: (15% annually) is slightly less than the actual average 1990s growth.
High growth: (20% annually) is half as fast as the growth rate from 2001 to 2002 in China, which was 40%.
Very high growth: There are as many vehicles per person in China in 2020 as there were in the United States in 2001.

Table 2.1
(continued)

Low efficiency: The fuel economy in China in 2020 is equal to U.S. average fuel economy in 2002.
Medium efficiency: 2% annual improvement in fuel efficiency until 2020.
High efficiency: Average fuel economy is twice what it currently is in the United States for light-duty vehicles (cars, SUVs, and light trucks combined) and approximately what commercially available hybrid-electric vehicles are in 2002.
Low miles: Fewer miles than currently driven on average each year in Japan.
Medium miles: The approximate number of miles currently driven each year in Japan.
High miles: The approximate number of miles currently driven each year in the United States.
Source: Author's calculations.

• The growth in Chinese automobile sales stays fairly constant from its average during the 1990s until 2020; and
• Either fuel efficiency improves or the number of miles driven is held to at least 5,000 miles per year. Table 2.1 shows that different combinations of levels of fuel economy and number of miles driven result in different amounts of total automotive oil consumption.

High-Growth Scenarios

China's automotive oil consumption could be large by 2030 if

• The annual rate of growth in the number of Chinese automobiles is 20 percent. Or, in a very high growth scenario, if there are as many cars per person in China in 2020 as there were in the United States in 2002; and
• The average fuel economy of Chinese cars in 2020 remains the same as the 2002 average fuel economy of U.S. cars; and
• Chinese drivers drive as far as U.S. drivers do each year. The resulting oil consumption from Chinese automobiles, in this highest-growth scenario, would be 24.8 million barrels per day.[2]

These scenarios illustrate that China's future oil consumption from automobiles is strongly dependent, at the very least, on how fast the automobile sector grows, how fuel efficient vehicles are in the future, and how far the cars are driven annually.

Aside from these three variables, there are other factors that will affect China's future oil consumption, such as the price of fuel, taxes and fees on automobile and road use, and the degree of usage of alternative methods of transportation. For the sake of comparison, it is helpful to look at other estimates of future Chinese oil consumption. The U.S. Energy Information Administration's International Energy Outlook 2002 projects China's total oil consumption (including automotive oil consumption) in 2020 to be between 7 and 12.8 million barrels per day, depending on the rate of China's economic growth (EIA 2002). Narrowing in on motor vehicles more specifically, a 2001 Argonne National Laboratory study estimated that Chinese vehicles would consume 225–330 million metric tons (about 4.5–6.6 million barrels per day) of oil by 2020 (He and Wang 2001). Similarly, a separate analysis forecasts Chinese automotive oil consumption in 2025 to range between 2.4 and 6.2 million barrels per day (Kobos, Erickson, and Drennen 2003).

There are also security dimensions to China's rising oil imports that not only affect China, but also many other countries in the world. If China becomes extremely dependent on oil from the Middle East, it will be forced to take a major security interest in a region that has long been of significant interest to the European Union, Japan, Russia, and the United States. This new interdependence will require close cooperation between China and each of these energy-consuming giants. China is also likely to become increasingly territorial about oil and gas reserves off its coast and in the South China Sea. The rights to some of these possible reserves have long been in dispute with some of China's neighbors.

Health and Environmental Dimensions of Automobiles in China

More people are killed and injured by automobiles in China than any-where else in the world, with 680 people killed and 45,000 injured *daily* ("Dream Machine" 2005). Other than accidents, the most immediate health and environmental problem related to automobiles in China is urban air pollution, although carbon emissions from automobiles in China will likely be a major source of global climate change in the future, absent aggressive policy intervention. There is increasing evidence that motor vehicles are now a leading cause of urban air pollution in China, which was not the case even a decade ago (Pan et al. 2004). Heating, cooking, power generation, and industrial coal consumption used to be the main contributors to urban air pollution, but during the 1990s, coal was replaced by natural gas in many urban buildings and homes.[3] Power plants are still a significant source of urban air pollution as well, but many plants are being relocated outside of the cities. Seven of the ten most polluted cities in the world are located in China, caused in great part by growing auto emissions. Monitoring data from 388 Chinese cities shows that only 31 percent can meet the Chinese standards for air quality (WHO 2004). Some city-specific data:

• In Beijing, the city where the 2008 Olympics are scheduled to take place, 92 percent of the carbon monoxide (CO) emissions, 94 percent of the hydrocarbon (HC) emissions, and 68 percent of the nitrogen oxide (NO_x) emissions are attributed to automobiles during the warm seasons. Even during the cold winter months, the majority of emissions come from automobiles (76 percent of CO, 94 percent of HC, 68 percent of NO_x) (GEF 2001).

• In Shanghai, vehicles are responsible for 90 percent of CO, 70 percent of HC, and 50 percent of NO_x emissions as of 1999 (interview with a representative of the Shanghai Science and Technology Commission 2002).

In general, mobile sources are estimated to account for 85 percent of CO emissions and 45 to 60 percent of NO_x emissions in typical Chinese cities (Walsh 2000). A recent study estimated that CO and HC emission factors for Chinese cars actually in use are five to ten times higher and that NO_x emission factors are two to five times higher than in developed countries (Fu et al. 2001).

The high emissions from autos in China are the result of inadequate emission-control regulations. Prior to 2000, emission standards for automobiles did not exist, leaded fuel was still widely used, and catalytic converters were not installed on cars. Starting in 2000, China banned the use of leaded fuels, required the installation of catalytic converters, required that all automobiles contain electronic fuel-injection engines, and adopted the European system for controlling automobile emissions. Beginning in 2000, all new automobiles had to be able to meet EURO I standards, which were required of European automobile manufacturers in 1992 (see table 2.2). Automobiles sold in the big cities, such as Beijing and Shanghai, were required to meet EURO II standards. In 2004, China required automobiles to meet EURO II standards, which was the

Table 2.2
Comparison of air-pollution emission standards for gasoline-fueled automobiles (grams/km)

Country, year	CO	HC	NOx	CO_2
Euro I, 1992	4.05	0.66	0.49	None
China, 2000	4.05	0.66	0.49	None
Euro II, 1994	3.28	0.34	0.25	None
China, 2004	3.28	0.34	0.25	None
Europe 1995[a]				187
U.S. Tier 1, current	2.6	0.16	0.37	None
Euro III, 2000	2.3	0.2	0.15	
China, 2007	2.3	0.2	0.15	None
Euro IV, 2005	1	0.1	0.08	
China, 2010	1	0.1	0.08	None
U.S. Tier 2, 2007[b]	1.3	0.01	0.04	None
Europe 2008[a]				140

[a] Separate and voluntary standard.
[b] There are different "emission bins" for the NO_x standard, but the fleet has to average at the number provided. There is an interim NO_x standard of 0.3 g/mile that eases the transition until 2007, and it is gradually being phased out between 2004 and 2007.
Data sources: Beardon 1999; EC 2001; interview with an official from the China State Environmental Protection Administration (SEPA), Cambridge, MA, 2002.

European level as of 1994. In 2005, automobiles sold in Beijing and Shanghai had to meet EURO III standards, and in 2007, the whole country is scheduled to go to EURO III levels. In 2010, EURO IV standards should take effect. Thus, Chinese air-pollution standards generally lag behind European levels by ten years, although more rapid progress is being made in some large coastal cities. Chinese standards for gasoline and diesel passenger cars lag behind U.S. levels even more, because air-pollution emission standards are still more stringent in the United States than in Europe, especially with respect to particulate emissions.

One of the biggest barriers to tightening vehicle emission standards in China is the poor fuel quality available in China. Although China eliminated lead from gasoline in 2000, sulfur levels remain high. When sulfur levels are elevated in fuels, the pollution-control equipment on vehicles can be rendered ineffective. Stringent emission standards thus require better emission-control technology used in tandem with cleaner fuels. To improve the quality of the fuels in China, major investments in refineries will be required, and until those refinery upgrades are achieved, it will be difficult to reduce conventional pollution from automobiles. The poor fuel quality in China has discouraged foreign vehicle manufacturers from transferring cleaner pollution-control technology because they have been reluctant to install more advanced technology if it cannot function properly due to the dirty fuels.

Most Chinese crude is considered "sweet" (low in sulfur) and so China's refineries were originally built to process the domestic low-sulfur crude. Now that China imports large quantities of oil from other countries, China finds itself without significant capacity to refine "sour" crude into low-sulfur products. As a result, sulfur levels in gasoline were estimated to be approximately 800 ppm, and 2,000 ppm for diesel throughout the country as of 2005, although considerable variation does exist. The city of Beijing required local refineries to produce lower-sulfur fuel by July 2005 (150 ppm for gasoline and 350 ppm for diesel), so that EURO III emission standards could be achieved in time for the 2008 Olympics.

One of China's most ambitious initiatives to address automobile pollution was the national Clean Vehicle Action program. This program was established in 1999 by SEPA and MOST with the target of having 10 percent of all taxis and 20 percent of all buses in twelve cities run on alternative fuels such as CNG or LPG by 2001. Although an estimated 129,000 alternative-fuel capable vehicles (AFVs) were on the road by May 2002 (most of them retrofits), it is not clear how many of them actually use the alternative fuels (Zhao 2002). In Shanghai, adoption of LPG fuel has been widespread among the taxis, because the government subsidized the price of LPG fuel to make it cheaper. Ninety percent of the 42,600 taxis in Shanghai are retrofitted VW Santanas, but astonishingly, one municipal official acknowledged in 2002 that most of these so-called clean vehicles did not even meet the basic EURO I standard because of a 30 percent increase in NO_x emissions (interview with a representative of the Shanghai Science and Technology Commission 2002). So, to the extent that the alternative-fueled vehicles cannot even meet the minimum air-pollution standards for regular automobiles, this program cannot be considered a success.

Another significant concern related to automobiles and the environment is carbon dioxide emissions, a potent greenhouse gas believed to cause global climate change (Watson 2001). Industrial and automotive emissions have already made China the second-largest emitter of greenhouse gases, after the United States. This environmental problem has less immediacy for China's citizens right now, because it does not directly affect them as obviously as the urban air pollution of particulates like NO_x, CO, and HC does. Over time, however, climate change will probably pose one of the biggest challenges to automobile use in China (and the rest of the world) because the transportation sector is typically one of the largest sources of greenhouse-gas emissions. The main way to reduce greenhouse-gas emissions from vehicles is through improving fuel efficiency, for carbon dioxide is a natural byproduct of burning gasoline in car engines. Unlike other common air pollutants, carbon emissions cannot be reduced by a catalytic converter in automobiles.

In 2004, the Chinese government approved the country's first fuel-efficiency standards for passenger cars. Concern about rising oil imports and energy security was the main motivation for the government to pass these standards. These standards took effect in July 2005 for all new passenger cars, SUVs, and MPVs with less than nine seats. There are separate standards for automatic and manual transmission vehicles. Unlike the Corporate Average Fuel Economy (CAFE) system in the United States, the Chinese issued maximum fuel-consumption limits for sixteen different weight classes. Standards will be tightened again in 2008, and at that point, it is estimated that most passenger cars weighing more than 3,500 pounds will not be able to meet the second phase of the standards without significant technological improvements (An et al. 2003). In other words, the 2008 version of the standards will be considerably more stringent than the U.S. CAFE standards as of 2005, especially for SUVs and light trucks. The goal of the Chinese government was to discourage the use of heavier, larger vehicles as individual passenger cars. On a fleetwide average basis, China's fuel-efficiency standards will be approximately 50 percent more stringent in 2008 than the U.S. CAFE standards in place in 2005, but less stringent than the equivalent Japanese or EU standards (An 2004).

The new fuel-efficiency standards are also likely to provoke transfer of more fuel-efficient technologies from foreign car manufacturers to China, although the standards are not so strict that they will motivate transfer of truly advanced technologies such as hybrid-electric cars.

To calculate potential carbon emissions in the future from China's passenger cars, the oil-consumption scenarios from earlier in the chapter were used to determine a range of possible carbon emissions from Chinese passenger cars in 2020. In the best-case scenario, if oil consumption was only 0.3 million barrels per day in 2020, annual carbon emissions from cars would be approximately 13 million metric tons. In the worse-case scenario, if oil consumption was 24 million barrels per day in 2020, annual carbon emissions from passenger cars would be approximately 1,051 million metric tons—one and a half times more than China's total carbon emissions in 2000. Using a midrange scenario of 3.3 million barrels of oil per day, annual carbon emissions from passenger cars in China in 2020 would be approximately 144 million metric tons.[4] Another study forecasts carbon emissions from Chinese passenger cars in 2025 to range between 89 and 231 million metric tons of carbon (Kobos, Erickson, and Drennen 2003).

As Chinese policymakers and research institutes develop additional fuel-efficiency standards in the future, they can learn from the mistakes in the U.S. experience. In the United States (like much of the world), transportation is the fastest-growing sector for energy consumption and greenhouse-gas emissions because fuel prices have remained relatively low and government regulations to reduce automotive fuel consumption have been stagnant for decades. Compounding the problem, Americans have taken a great liking to the gas-guzzling large SUVs and pickup trucks, driving them farther and farther each year partly because of the persistently low gas prices. As a result, the average fuel consumption of U.S. automobiles has not improved in years.

Because Chinese consumers have limited disposable income, they rate fuel economy among their top concerns when purchasing an automobile. Chinese-consumer concern provides the main incentive for auto manufacturers to produce more fuel-efficient cars at this time in China. GM actually introduced a more fuel-efficient Buick luxury sedan, for example, to make its product more competitive in China (interview with

P. Murtaugh, chair and CEO, China Group, General Motors China, Shanghai, 2002). No other foreign manufacturer claims to have improved the fuel efficiency of any auto models once they have been put into production in China. On the other hand, GM and American Motors Corporation (now DaimlerChrysler) introduced two inefficient SUVs to China: the Jeep Cherokee (Beijing Jeep) and the Chevrolet Blazer (Jinbei GM). On the bright side, U.S. manufacturers have also introduced several relatively fuel efficient cars as well, such as the Ford Fiesta and Buick Sail.

In summary, there are numerous energy and environmental implications of increased passenger-car use in China. Passenger cars are already causing a number of problems, including increased urban air pollution, emissions of greenhouse gases, and oil consumption and imports. The Chinese automobile industry, however, is an important sector in the Chinese economy, and it contributes positively to economic growth, to job creation, and to the development of national technological capabilities, as is discussed in the next chapter. Ideally, the problems can be diminished and the benefits enhanced through effective public-policy measures and the contributions of foreign investors.

3

Zoom, Zoom, Zoom: The Auto Industry and Economic Development

The automobile industry that emerged during the 1990s in China has greatly contributed to economic growth in that country. Chinese government policy and foreign direct investment both played important roles in the transformation of yesterday's backward, small, weak industry with few capabilities to today's industry—the third-largest in the world as of 2005. At this time, the main contributions of the auto industry to the Chinese economy are in terms of output and employment, but it is not clear that this industry has gained skills beyond manufacturing, parts localization, and limited design capabilities. Inconsistent and occasionally weak Chinese government policies, the lack of incentives for foreign manufacturers to teach their Chinese counterparts more about technology and design, and China's entry into the WTO have all combined to limit the potential of this industry. Still, the Chinese automobile market has proven itself to be the most dynamic and explosive in the world during the last decade and the potential exists for this growth to continue virtually unabated.

The Chinese Economy

China's economy is now about one-tenth the size of the U.S. economy with a GDP of US$1.6 trillion in 2004, when converted at market exchange rates. In purchasing-power-parity terms, however, China's economy is now $7.5 trillion, two-thirds the size of the U.S. economy (World Bank 2002).[1] The Chinese economy is among the world's fastest growing, with an average annual growth rate between 1994 and 2004 of 9.0 percent (Economist Intelligence Unit 2005). During the past twenty years, an estimated 208 million people in China have been lifted out of poverty, and, according to the Chinese government, the total number of people living in poverty there was reduced to 42 million in 1999 (Xinhua 1999).[2] A major driver of this impressive economic performance has been the development of China's manufacturing sector.

The structure of the Chinese economy has changed significantly during the past twenty years as well, as can be seen in table 3.1. In 1983, agriculture accounted for 33 percent of the value added by the Chinese economy, but this sector had contracted to only 15 percent of value added by 2003. In contrast, industrial development (including manufacturing) and services surged during this period in China, together accounting for only 67 percent of value added in 1983 but rising to 85 percent of value added in 2003.

The Central Role of the Auto Industry in Economic Development

In 1994, the Chinese government designated the automobile industry one of the "pillar" industries of economic development. Undoubtedly, the Chinese government's decision to make the automobile sector a mainstay of the economy greatly contributed to economic development in China, especially with respect to employment and output. There were 1.6 million Chinese employed by this industry as of 2003.[3] The value added by the Chinese auto industry represented 6 percent of the total value added of manufacturing in China in 2003, a near doubling of this percentage from its level in 1990 (CATARC 2004a).

Table 3.1
Structure of the Chinese economy: Value added (percent GDP)

	1983	1993	2003
Agriculture	33	30	15
Industry	45	47	52
Manufacturing (included in Industry)	*37*	*35*	*39*
Services	22	33	33

Source: World Bank, World Development Indicators database, 2005b.

During the 1990s, China received more foreign direct investment than any other developing country (US$38.4 billion in 2000 alone) as investors sought to reap some of the gains of China's fast-growing economy.[4] Much of this foreign investment in China was in the automobile industry. At the beginning of 2001, it was estimated that there were more than 800 Chinese companies in automotive-related industries that had received foreign direct investment (FDI), and this investment was valued at US$12 billion (Zhang 2002).

FDI in the automobile sector has contributed to the economic success of this industry in China in a number of ways. First, it has created desirable and stable jobs for Chinese workers in the joint-venture firms. Second, this investment has strongly benefited the wider economy because the Sino-foreign joint ventures have created a strong source of demand in China for raw materials and automotive parts and components. In 1994, the Chinese government imposed "localization" requirements on the Sino-foreign joint ventures, which forced them to use a certain percentage of Chinese-made parts in their automobiles. Many of the Chinese suppliers were initially unable to meet the standards of the foreign firms, so the foreigners worked with Chinese suppliers to improve the quality of their products. Once the suppliers learned how to enhance their products, they began to export them to other markets, which allowed them to expand production and lower unit costs. Overall, these "backward linkages" from the Sino-foreign joint ventures and the Chinese automobile industry in general are increasingly contributing to economic growth in China. By the mid-1990s, the Chinese auto industry was providing the demand for 5–6 percent of total steel production, 80–90 percent of petroleum products, 14–16 percent of machine-tool production, 50 percent of tempered-glass production, 45 percent of tire production, 15 percent of engineered-plastics production, and 15 percent of paint production (CATARC 2001).

On the other hand, it has been shown that in general, FDI is not always positive for the receiving developing country. For example, a World Bank study noted that foreign investment does not necessarily stimulate new economic development because FDI is often attracted to the already productive sources of the economy, not the less productive ones (Saggi

2002). Perversely, there appears to be an inverse correlation of domestic skill formation with regard to foreign investment in developing countries: *high* levels of FDI are associated with *low* levels of domestic skill formation (Amsden 2001).

There is some evidence that FDI in the Chinese automobile industry has indeed reduced the incentive for indigenous Chinese technological innovation, and this may hurt the economic prospects of the industry in the longer term. At this time, Chinese companies are still basically reliant on their foreign partners for advanced technology. But foreign firms cannot bear the entire brunt of the blame because the Chinese government's policies toward the sector have been inconsistent and sometimes contradictory, as is discussed in more detail below and in chapter 4. Moreover, local governments, who own most of the Chinese auto companies, have been resistant to central-government intervention.

The Structure of the Chinese Auto Industry

As of 2005, twelve foreign-invested joint ventures dominated the Chinese domestic passenger-car market, with about a hundred small firms on the periphery. The foreign-invested joint ventures accounted for most of China's passenger-car production. In 2002, there was a major merger within the Chinese automobile industry when Tianjin Automobile Xiali Company (TAIC), which had formed a joint venture with Toyota, merged with First Auto Works to form Tianjin FAW Xiali Corporation Ltd. Therefore, as can be seen in appendix C, there are currently twelve major Sino-foreign joint ventures: Shanghai VW, FAW-Volkswagen, Shanghai GM, Dongfeng Citroën, Dongfeng Nissan, Dongfeng Kia, Guangzhou Honda, Chang'An Suzuki, Chang'An Ford, Beijing Jeep, Beijing Hyundai, and FAW-Tianjin-Toyota.

China's Entry into the WTO

China became the 143rd member of the World Trade Organization (WTO) in 2001, and its entry is already forcing its manufacturers to "sink or swim" in the international market. To become a member of the WTO, China had to negotiate a bilateral concession agreement with any member country that requested one, as well as negotiate a multilateral protocol of accession with all WTO members as a group. Not surprisingly, the United States requested a bilateral concession agreement from China, and these negotiations became known as the Permanent Normal Trading Relations (PNTR) negotiations in the United States. The negotiations were so named because if China entered the WTO, the U.S. Congress would be required to stop its annual review of Most-Favored Nation (MFN) status. Any provisions that China agreed with any individual country automatically would apply to all WTO member countries because of the WTO's nondiscrimination rules (WTO 2003a).

The PNTR agreement was concluded in November 1999, upheld by the U.S. House of Representatives in May 2000, and passed by the U.S. Senate in September 2000. Entering into force in November 2000, the PNTR agreement contained many specific concessions regarding the automobile industry in China. First, it specified that import tariffs for complete automobiles would be reduced from 80–100 to 25 percent by July 1, 2006. Import tariffs for parts and components would be reduced from 35 to 10 percent by the same date. Import quotas on automobiles would be decreased 15 percent per year until they are canceled in 2005. Import licenses would also be phased out by 2005. On China's accession to the WTO, non-Chinese bank financial institutions would be permitted to provide financing for automobiles without any limitations.

Also on accession, China would no longer condition importation or investment approvals on whether any competing domestic suppliers exist, or on performance requirements of any kind, such as export performance, local content, technology transfer, offsets, foreign-exchange balancing, or research and development. Foreign and domestic businesses would be taxed uniformly, and majority ownership limits on foreign manufacturers for engines would also be eliminated (ITA 2003a). Also, provincial governments would be given the authority to approve FDI projects up to US$150 million by 2005. Until 2002 when it was raised to US$60 million, the limit was US$30 million, giving the central government great influence over the terms of FDI agreements (Huang 2002).

The European Union also negotiated a concession agreement with specific provisions for the automobile industry, namely, that foreign investors would be allowed to have a majority share in engine joint-venture manufacturing operations, and that joint ventures would be allowed to change the production mix without government approval. In the past, the government restricted the number of models that a given company was allowed to produce (Ali et al. 2005).

The Effect of the WTO

Most of the Sino-foreign joint ventures frantically spent the early years of the twenty-first century trying to improve the quality and price of their cars while there was still some government protection left. For the Chinese manufacturers who did not have foreign partners, the outlook became daunting because most could not even compete in the protected domestic market against the Sino-foreign joint-venture firms.[5] As a result of China's entry into the WTO, the State Council's Development Research Center had estimated that there would be a 15 percent reduction in auto industry output, a 14.5 percent reduction in employment, a 105 percent increase in imports, and a 7.8 percent reduction in exports (Li and Wang 1998; Ali et al. 2005). The assumption was that many of the domestic firms without foreign affiliations would fail to compete, which would cause significant unemployment and labor-market dislocations regionally. In reality, the reduction in output did not occur because sales surged due to the lower prices brought on by the competition induced by the WTO. Similarly, there was no reduction in employment. Imports did surge, but not as much as many had expected, and exports of passenger cars have remained weak (only 10,000 in 2004) due to the relatively high cost and poor quality of cars produced in China (Bremer 2005).

The new competition spurred many changes within the industry, with some companies losing significant market share (e.g., Volkswagen) and new companies emerging in the marketplace (McGregor 2002). Price wars broke out at the beginning of 2002, and continued to rage through 2005 (Xinhua Economic News Service 2002; Kurtenbach 2005). The restructuring and consolidation of the industry that the Chinese government had long sought (see chapter 4) began to be realized as companies started to merge to enhance competitiveness. The most notable merger was between First Auto Works and Tianjin Xiali Auto Industry Corporation, which formed a joint venture with Toyota Motor Corporation.

Meanwhile, the Chinese government has also discovered creative mechanisms consistent with its WTO obligations that help to support its domestic industry. On January 1, 2005, China abolished the car import quota system as required by the WTO, but replaced it with an automatic import licensing system, which allows it to monitor the number of imports of vehicles and components. In the new system, applicants for the import of auto products for sale must submit dealer-authorization certificates or business licenses (Trade Development Council 2005). The government hopes that this policy will reduce the number of car dealers and strengthen the management of the sales channels for automobiles, because not all dealers will be granted licenses to import cars (Asia Pulse 2005).

The Chinese government also issued a new regulation in April 2005 on the importation of automotive parts and components. Under China's WTO obligations, prior local content requirements were abolished on entry, and import tariffs for complete automobiles were to be reduced to 25 percent by July 1, 2006, and to 10 percent for parts and components. The new rules impose the same tariff for imports of certain combinations of key components as is allowed to be imposed on completed vehicles. For example, importing complete knockdown (CKD) kits, or engines along with three or more of a combination of transmissions, driving axles, chassis, steering systems, braking systems, or air conditioners, would be assessed a tariff equal to that of a complete vehicle (Asia Pulse 2005; People's Daily 2005). This new rule is designed to motivate automakers to increase the local content of cars manufactured in China. Japan urged China not to introduce this new system, and has warned that the new rules may violate GATT Article II (Schedule of Concession) (METI 2005).

It is certainly in the Chinese government's interest to ensure that its automobile industry survives China's entry into the WTO. The U.S. auto industry claims that auto manufacturers and related industries provide one out of every seven American jobs (including jobs dependent on the industry) and contribute 5 percent of annual "private-sector GDP" to the U.S. economy (Alliance of Automobile Manufacturers 2003). Some of the Chinese partners in auto joint ventures have acquired respectable product-manufacturing capabilities, but they still lack design capabilities and have not yet achieved technological independence. Unshielded exposure to the international market will probably condemn China's domestic auto manufacturers to technological foreign reliance unless the government can devise alternative methods to build up local technological and business skills and thereby give Chinese manufacturers more bargaining and market power.

If China cannot develop its own capabilities, it will lose the many contributions that the auto industry could potentially make to Chinese economic development. Cars assembled in China with foreign technology will help retain employment and tax revenue from sales. If Chinese auto manufacturers could somehow become leaders in their own right without using technology transfer in the joint ventures, however, a greater share of the profits (that would otherwise be lost to the foreign companies) could be retained and reinvested in developing more capabilities in the auto sector. While this emergence of a strong, self-sufficient Chinese auto industry is not plausible in the short term, a middle-ground solution for China would be to find incentives to make the foreign companies commit to the joint ventures more heartily, reinvest their profits, train Chinese workers more thoroughly, and view China as a potential source of innovative ideas.

The Economic Costs of the Chinese Auto Industry

As important as the automobile industry is to China's economic development, the environmental and security-related costs of automobile use may offset some of the economic benefits. State Environmental Protection Agency (SEPA) Minister Xie Zhenhua has stated that the costs of air and water pollution to China's economy could equal 4 to 8 percent of annual GDP (U.S. Embassy Beijing 2000). Air pollution from motor vehicles is a growing source of these costs.

In addition, the economic costs of substantial oil imports cannot be ignored. These economic costs include the actual costs of oil imports, the effect of increased demand on world oil prices, and the potential reduction in domestic economic productivity due to higher energy input costs.

Oil imports themselves are already expensive for China. According to the Economist Intelligence Unit, imported petroleum (and related products) cost China US$15.6 billion in 2002, making petroleum-related imports the fourth-largest category of import behind industrial machinery, textiles, and electrical machinery (EIU DataServices 2003).[6] In January 2003, China posted its first trade deficit since 1996, and the Chinese government attributed most of this deficit to the higher price of imported oil. At the same time, the Chinese government announced that it intended to build a strategic petroleum reserve, which is estimated to cost US$10 billion over ten years (Markus 2003). If China became a huge importer of oil, world oil prices would probably rise in response to such a vast increase in demand, which would have economic repercussions in many oil-importing countries.

Noting that conventional market forces do not determine the international supply of oil, Bohi and Montgomery (1982) argue that there are three "destabilizing effects" of increased world oil prices. First, increased oil prices can cause an increase in the amount of wealth transferred abroad. Second, they can reduce domestic production of goods and services as a consequence of lower oil consumption. Third, increased oil prices can reduce total domestic output, because nonoil market prices cannot adjust efficiently to the higher price of oil. A study of the causes of the U.S. economic recession during the 1970s supports the second effect identified by Bohi and Montgomery. "The slowdown of sectoral productivity growth after 1973 is partly a consequence of the sharp increase in the price of energy relative to other productive inputs," and "the fall in sectoral productivity growth after 1973 is the primary explanation for the decline in productivity for the U.S. economy as a whole" (Jorgenson 1982, 27). Yet the potential economic cost of an oil shock can be offset for an oil-importing country if the oil-exporting countries (i.e., Organization of Petroleum Exporting Countries) buy more goods and services from the importing country using their increased revenue from the higher oil prices. It has been shown, however, that in practice, OPEC producers typically initially spend only a fraction of their additional oil income (Lienert 1982). Finally, some believe that an increase in the price of imported oil can affect the value of the currency of the oil-importing country (Banks 1980).

In conclusion, this chapter provides an overview of China's historic economic growth in recent decades. The auto industry has played a strong role in this growth, even defying predictions that the sector would lag after China's entry to the WTO. Foreign direct investment into the auto sector has been tremendous, and growth in passenger-car output and employment has been unprecedented. But despite some creative efforts to exploit the narrow openings in WTO rules to enhance endogenous production capabilities in the domestic auto sector, it is not clear that the Chinese government has managed to find a way to channel FDI so as to produce real learning and improvements in Chinese technological capabilities that will sustain broad-based growth in this sector over the long term.

4

Foreign Technology in the Development of China's Automotive Sector

Foreign technology has influenced the development of China's automobile sector since its inception, but foreign influence has been most pronounced during the last decade, the only period of substantial growth in the history of this sector. In 1963, China produced a grand total of eleven cars; twenty years later, China was still producing fewer than 10,000 passenger cars per year (Harwit 1995). Another twenty years later in 2002, with the auto market raging "like the burning fire in winter," Chinese auto companies collectively produced a million cars for the first time (NBS 2002).

To make this profound transformation from producing eleven cars in 1963 to the current two million or more annually, China had to quickly acquire the necessary knowledge and technological capabilities for automobile production. Starting all over again after the Cultural Revolution from practically nothing in the way of equipment and know-how, China was faced with a classic "make or buy" technology dilemma. Should it try to develop these capabilities internally, or was it too far behind the world leaders for this ever to be feasible? What could China hope to obtain from foreign providers of technology? A historical perspective reveals that the Chinese government has been highly inconsistent regarding these questions.

Initially, the Chinese government was forced to buy technology and tried to license automotive technology from the Japanese, but after those models entered production the technology stagnated and was not updated. In the early 1980s, China negotiated its first two joint ventures with foreign auto companies: American Motor Corporation (AMC) and Volkswagen. The AMC joint venture, known as Beijing Jeep, struggled (see chapter 5) more than VW, but the technology-transfer process in the joint ventures did not yield significantly more than the licensing arrangements had in terms of the transfer of knowledge and know-how, for reasons discussed in more detail later. It was not until 1994 that the Chinese government actually articulated a clear strategy for the industry. Four years later, however, China reversed many of these policies in its accession agreement with the United States for entry into the WTO.

Amsden (2001) provides a typology of technological capabilities that developing-country industries must acquire to become competitive in the world market: production, project execution, and innovation capabilities.[1] Production capabilities include being able to oversee the operation of established facilities, production engineering, repair and maintenance of physical capital, troubleshooting, and adaptation of products and processes as needed. Project-execution capabilities include personnel training, preproject feasibility studies, project management, project engineering, procurement, plant construction, and start-up of operations. Innovation capabilities include the skills necessary to create new processes and products (ranging from basic science to product development).

After World War II, and then again after the Cultural Revolution, China lacked all of the automotive capabilities described above: Chinese firms had no production, no project execution, and no innovation capabilities at all. This chapter will describe how, historically, China has sought to acquire these capabilities from foreigners. A chronology of automobile industry–related events is available in appendix B.

Prewar Infancy

An important prerequisite for successful economic development in "late-industrializing" countries like China was the acquisition of manufacturing experience before World War II. Such long-term manufacturing experience provided many obvious benefits for late-industrializing countries and also built confidence among foreigners that their investment would pay off (Amsden 2001). Just before World War II, pockets of manufacturing expertise cropped up along the eastern coast of China.

These areas were most concentrated in northeast China (known then as Manchuria and under Japanese control from 1931) and in the handful of free-market "treaty ports" carved out by foreigners (Fairbank 1951). The manufacturing experience that accumulated in these areas in China was closely linked with the knowledge brought by the Japanese in Manchuria and the Europeans (especially the British) and Americans in the treaty ports. To cite one example, in the 1930s, historic mining centers in northeast China inspired the Japanese to develop China's first heavy-industry complex during their occupation of Manchuria, including the mining industries of coal, iron ore, and oil shale, as well as large-scale factories for the production of iron, steel, industrial machinery, and transportation equipment (Rawski 1989). Chinese workers in these factories began to accumulate knowledge about how to produce such products.

With respect to the automobile sector in particular, China had meager prewar manufacturing experience. In the early twentieth century, automobiles initially were imported from abroad, mostly from the United States. Imports served the Shanghai market and were driven by the Chinese business and political elite. For example, famous revolutionaries Sun Yat-sen and Zhou Enlai were both known to have driven Buicks during that time. It was expensive for foreigners to ship these products to China, so parts-and-components companies sprang up in Beijing, Tianjin, and Shanghai to provide some elements of the automobiles, such as the heavy bodies. This development led to the construction of a few crude assembly plants to put these Chinese-made parts together with the other imported components (Harwit 1995). Predictably, these three cities later became centers of automotive expertise in the late twentieth century. For the most part, however, foreign auto companies did not invest in China during the early twentieth century to the extent they did in other developing countries. For example, GM built an assembly plant in India in 1928 and another in Brazil in 1929 but merely opened company offices in Shanghai that same year.

Meanwhile, some Chinese companies were acquiring manufacturing experience in other sectors that they would later apply to the automobile sector. One current Chinese manufacturer, Chang'An Automobile (Group) Corp. was originally founded as the Shanghai Western-Style

Artillery Bureau in 1862. It was established as part of the Qing Dynasty's "westernization" experiment, and its artillery was used during China's war of resistance against Japan. The company was moved three times, from Shanghai to Suzhou, then to Nanjing, and eventually to its current location in the western city of Chongqing. Using its experience with artillery production, Chang'An gradually began producing other types of machinery, and was renamed the State-Owned Chang'An Machine Building Plant in 1953. The plant produced its first automobile in 1958 using technology imported from the Soviet Union.[2]

Before World War II, most foreign companies were content to export automobiles to China. For example, although Dr. Sun Yat-sen wrote to Henry Ford in 1924 asking him to help build an automobile industry in China, Ford merely opened a sales and service branch in Shanghai. In his letter to Ford, Sun Yat-sen wrote, "I have . . . read of your remarkable work in America. And I think you can do similar work in China on a much vaster and significant scale. It is my sense that your work in America has been more individual and personal, whereas here in China you would have an opportunity to express and embody your mind and ideals in the enduring form of a new industrial system" (quoted in Ford 2002, 2).

For its part, the Chinese government appeared to be content to import automobiles from abroad due to its lack of real initiative to establish a domestic industry at that time. To be sure, the Chinese government was in constant turmoil during the first half of the twentieth century (Fairbank 1951). This was a time of inconsistent policy and little economic development in China, indeed chaos, because of leadership struggles and successions, the war with Japan during the 1930s, and then the long civil war in concert with World War II.

The Early Postwar Years

After the triumph of Chairman Mao Zedong's Communist revolution, Chinese society began a radical transformation through industrialization. China relied heavily on its northern neighbor and ally, the Soviet Union, for technical assistance. The People's Republic of China (PRC) decided it wanted to develop an automobile industry for the purposes of transporting rural products and the military. Thus, the Soviets transferred the first real automotive knowledge and hard technology to China. They are known, for example, to have helped start China's First Auto Works (FAW) in 1953 in the northeastern city of Changchun, where there were remnants of manufacturing infrastructure left behind by the Japanese. The first product produced by FAW was the *Jiefang* (liberation) truck, a version of the Soviet ZIS 150 model (Harwit 1995). The Soviets also transferred the design for a smaller all-terrain utility vehicle to China, following up with careful training of Chinese workers to ensure that they could actually manufacture the design. Amazingly, this same basic design—dating back half a century—is still in production at the joint venture between DaimlerChrysler and Beijing Jeep.

Regarding passenger cars, FAW produced its first *Hongqi* (Red Flag) black sedans, based on Daimler Benz's 200 model, in 1958 to serve as limousines for the government elite. Also in 1958, Shanghai Automotive Assembly Plant (now Shanghai Automotive Industry Corporation— SAIC) produced its first passenger car, the Phoenix. These developments suddenly stopped after the Sino-Soviet split of 1960 halted all foreign technology transfer and assistance for the Chinese automobile sector for a crucial *two decades*, years in which the Japanese and Korean auto manufacturers built up their own indigenous capacity to challenge the North Atlantic automobile firms. Indeed, Japanese firms were not all that far ahead of the Chinese at that time; Nissan produced only 865 passenger cars in 1950 (Halberstam 1986).

Stunted Development

Even before the 1960 Sino-Soviet split, automotive industrial development was hindered by central government policies, especially the Great Leap Forward campaign (1958–1960). Instead of consolidating companies and taking advantage of economies of scale with mass production, as European and American auto companies were doing, the Chinese government's aim (against the advice of the Soviets) was to stimulate a small-scale industrialization of all the rural areas. This approach proved to be unfeasible and ultimately caused a huge famine. But a related tradition of small-scale enterprise endures in the automotive sector in China, which might explain why there are still 118 passenger-car manufacturers, some of which are very small, still operating to this day around the country.

After the Great Leap Forward, the "Third Front" campaign was promulgated to promote self-reliance and develop an inland industrial and military base beginning in 1964. During the Third Front years, heavy industry was decentralized and dispersed around the country to make factories more resistant to attack. Entire factories were torn down and rebuilt in remote mountainous regions. By 1969, there were 33 automobile factories producing a grand total of 150 cars (Harwit 1995). As many as half the Third Front factories are still in place, including the Shiyan Number Two Automobile Factory in Hubei province (Shapiro 2001), later known as Second Auto Works (SAW) and currently known as Dongfeng Automobile Company. The remote Sichuan and Shanxi Auto Works companies also began construction of factories in this period. All of these factories produced primarily medium-sized trucks (Zhang 2002).

Production of passenger cars essentially ceased during the Cultural Revolution (1966–1971), when there was no investment in the automobile industry. Sedans were regarded as luxury articles, so they were not produced, and most factories entirely shut down their automobile production (FBIS 1994). SAW began construction of its factory in 1967, but it did not start operation until 1975. Chang'An completely stopped producing its cross-country vehicle in 1962 and shifted to the manufacture of other goods. According to government statistics, there was also no investment at all in the automobile industry during the 1970s (CATARC 2002a). Coincidentally, these were the golden years of the U.S. automobile market, a time when U.S. auto plants were each producing 200,000–400,000 units a year. Meanwhile, all of China's automobile factories combined produced less than 700 automobiles annually during that same time (Harwit 1995). The lost opportunity to the Chinese in terms of auto-industry-related technological and economic development was probably enormous. All this time, while the Europeans, Americans, and Japanese were producing hundreds of thousands of automobiles each year, profiting and "learning by doing" to increase their innovation capabilities, the development of Chinese manufacturers was stunted. For example, during the 1950s, the U.S. automobile industry represented nearly 20 percent of the gross national product of the United States (Halberstam 1986).

A Second Infancy

China's automobile industry experienced a second infancy after China reopened its doors to the world after the Cultural Revolution in the late 1970s. For years, automobile production had essentially been at a standstill. Not only had expertise been forgotten or lost, but there had been no development of new technologies, cultivation of skilled and innovative workers, or acquisition of technological capacity since the 1960s. Realizing that they needed automobiles, but not wanting to become totally reliant on imports, China's government imposed restrictions on auto imports and reached out to foreign companies through technology licensing and the formation of joint ventures. Initially, China asked the Japanese for help. The Japanese exported a large number of trucks and agreed to provide some technical assistance to the Chinese during the early 1970s (Harwit 1995). But the Japanese were wary of generating potential competitors to their own automobile companies, so the extent and duration of their technology transfer was limited.

The first major manufacturing joint venture of any kind to be established between a Chinese company and a foreign firm after the Cultural Revolution was an automotive joint venture. This was the Beijing Jeep Corporation (BJC) joint venture signed between state-owned Beijing Automobile Industry Corporation (BAIC) and American Motors Corporation (AMC) in January 1984 (see chapter 5). In this joint venture, AMC was to provide all the new technology for Beijing Jeep. The Chinese government had decided to limit foreign ownership to no more than 50 percent for automobile joint ventures, and AMC duly took a minority stake. For this first joint venture, technology was transferred in the form of "complete knockdown" (CKD) kits. CKDs are sets of automotive parts that are packaged in one country, then exported to another for assembly. For the Beijing Jeep joint venture, Jeep Cherokee CKD kits were packaged in the United States by AMC, sold to Beijing Jeep, and then exported to China for assembly by the BJC Chinese workers.

Shortly after the establishment of Beijing Jeep, a second joint venture was established between the Shanghai Automotive Industry Corporation (SAIC) and Volkswagen in October 1984. Volkswagen took a 50 percent stake. In the long run, Shanghai VW has proved to be much more successful than Beijing Jeep. It has been by far the largest annual producer of passenger cars since the mid-1980s.

Chinese auto companies also licensed technology from foreign firms in these nascent years. One prime example is acquisition of technology for the ubiquitous compact cars used as taxis in many large cities. Tianjin Automotive Industry Corporation (TAIC) licensed technology from Daihatsu in 1986 to produce the *Xiali* (Charade) minisedan often seen in use as red taxis in Beijing and Tianjin. In another example, Chang'An licensed technology from Suzuki in 1983 to produce its own minicar, which is also used as the yellow taxi in Chongqing (Chang'An Automobile Group 2002). These subcompact sedans are still in production today, virtually unchanged from their original model.

To help create a market for these new automobile joint ventures, the Chinese government officially permitted private ownership of automobiles starting in 1984. For at least the first decade thereafter, however, government officials would provide most of the demand for new automobiles.

Trying to Learn from Foreigners

After the flurry of activity in the 1980s, the government began to reconsider its automotive industrial strategy. China had not gained much knowledge from the foreign firms, which essentially selected what would be transferred and how, without necessarily teaching their Chinese partners anything significant. The only real requirement for the foreign companies was to get the technology into production, and there were no specific stipulations on technology transfer. For example, while the government wished to increase the production and availability of passenger cars, as late as 1990 few were actually being produced. At this time, the output of automobiles still only accounted for less than 10 percent of total motor-vehicle output (Zhang 2002).

Meanwhile, two new joint ventures were formed: one in 1990 between VW and First Auto Works, to produce Jettas, and the other between French Citroën and Second Auto Works (now Dongfeng Motor Corporation), to produce the *Fukang* compact in 1992.

There were many differing views within the government at this time about whether China should try to foster its own domestic industry or whether it was too late for China to possibly catch up with the foreigners. After all, if the foreigners were willing to manufacture and sell the cars in China, then at least China benefited from the jobs and tax revenues associated with those joint ventures. Yet there were those who believed that China should model itself after the Japanese and Koreans, who had both managed to develop world-class automobile companies after World War II that were now challenging or even surpassing the U.S. and European companies.

1994 Auto Policy

China's government officials finally came to agreement and issued the first real industrial policy for the automobile industry in 1994, more than ten years after the announcement of the first joint venture and subsequent formation of three other major joint ventures. This policy took a radically different approach from the de facto policy of the 1980s in three ways:

1. *Consolidation.* The new policy sought to consolidate the dozens of automobile companies into a few powerhouse firms akin to the "Big Three" model in the United States. More precisely, the Chinese government was striving for a "Big Three, Mini Three" (*San Da, San Xiao*— three big firms and three smaller firms) arrangement and it intended to focus most of its own energies and investment on those six companies.

2. *Protectionism and technology transfer.* The Chinese government also decided to protect all manufacturers located in China (including the joint ventures) from international competition by establishing import quotas and stiff tariffs (80–100 percent) on both vehicles and parts. It continued to limit foreign ownership in joint ventures to 50 percent to give the Chinese partners more control and bargaining power. Another major change was the placement of specific requirements on foreign investors.

For example, all joint ventures must localize their parts and components by at least 40 percent (and powerful incentives were created to go beyond compliance). Foreign firms vying for new joint ventures were asked to transfer more knowledge to their partners, and they were told to establish joint technical centers for training Chinese workers.

3. *Market creation.* To stimulate the market, the government reaffirmed its encouragement of private ownership for passenger cars. As noted, China officially permitted the private ownership of vehicles in 1984.

These new requirements did not seem to deter the next foreign investors in China in the least. After the 1994 policy was issued, almost every big multinational automobile firm bid on a project to establish a joint venture with Shanghai Auto Industry Corporation, considered by many to be the best Chinese passenger-car firm. In the end, General Motors made the largest single foreign investment ever in China as of 1997 when it established its joint venture, as discussed in detail in the case study on Shanghai GM in chapter 6. Also in 1997, Honda took over Peugeot's troubled joint venture with Guangzhou Automotive Manufacturing Company, and then Ford entered into negotiations with Chang'An in 1999. There was a veritable flood of investment into the Chinese auto industry during the 1990s from both Chinese government and foreign sources. According to government statistics, total investment into the motor-vehicle and related industries from all sources totaled nearly US$60 billion during the 1990s. To put this in perspective, total investment in the vehicle sector from 1953 to 1989 equaled only US$1 billion, and 88 percent of that amount was invested during the mid- to late 1980s (CATARC 2002b).

Rapid Growth but Continuing Small Scale

Although both domestic and foreign investment in China's automobile industry began in earnest during the 1980s, substantial growth in production and sales did not occur until the mid-1990s. As late as 1991, only 81,055 cars were produced by the entire industry, but this number doubled in 1992 and continued to grow rapidly. During the 1990s, the average annual growth rate of passenger-car production was 27 percent. In other words, passenger-car production was doubling about every two and a half years. Preliminary reports for 2002 suggest a 40 percent increase in total production over 2001 levels. For a few companies, the growth has been even more dramatic. As of December 2002, sales had grown 43 percent for FAW-VW, 67 percent for SAIC-Chery, 91 percent for Shanghai GM, and 57 percent for Dongfeng Citroën (CATARC 2003).

It is easy to be impressed by such numbers because new retail automobile sales in the United States grew on average only 0.3 percent each year during the 1990s (Davis and Diegel 2002). But total production numbers remind observers that the industry is still young. In 2000, only 612,000 cars were produced in China compared with the 17.2 million new cars that were registered in the United States, and the total automobile stock is still very small in China. By the end of 2001, there were only an estimated 8.5 million passenger cars in China compared with 179 million in the United States (including SUVs). Many automobile companies in China still produce fewer than 100,000 automobiles a year.

In retrospect, the 1994 automobile-industry policy had mixed results. The consolidation of the automobile industry into a handful of big firms was not realized. Instead of 6 major firms, there are still 13 out of a total of 118 total manufacturers. The high degree of protection given to the industry by the government was not repaid by concerted and effective efforts within the industry to become more competitive in the world market. Fewer-than-expected automobiles are being exported to foreign markets, and all producers worry about whether they can compete against the flood of imports expected now that China has joined the WTO. Today, only a handful of passenger cars are actually exported from the country and of those exports, the majority go to developing countries, although in 2002, 256 Chinese cars were actually exported to the United States through American Automobile Network Holdings (Ibison and McGregor 2002). Most manufacturers in China ruefully admit that their cars are much more expensive than and of inferior quality to the foreign competition. According to GM China's Philip Murtaugh, "We have no plans whatsoever to export to Europe or North America. We're not (cost) competitive with cars produced in North America or Europe" (quoted in Zoia 2001, 37).

On the other hand, the 1994 policy effectively forced manufacturers to use a high percentage of Chinese-made parts and components, creating thriving related industries. For example, in 1994 only 24 percent of the VW Jetta parts were made by Chinese companies, but by 2000, 84 percent of the parts were Chinese-made (Huang 2002).

Thrust into the Unfettered Free Market

China entered the World Trade Organization (WTO) in 2001. When China began liberalizing its trade barriers because of its entry into the WTO, the Chinese automobile industry was expected to undergo more upheaval than any other sector of the Chinese economy with the exception of agriculture, which was projected to lose 9.6 million workers (Li and Wang 1998). This projection was due to the fact that highly protected sectors like agriculture and automobiles would contract significantly, while labor-intensive open sectors such as textiles and clothing would be the main beneficiaries.

As of 2005, it was too early to make a definitive assessment about whether entry into the WTO helped or hurt China's auto industry. Given the state-owned Chinese firms' historical resistance to reform and change, the government decision to enter may have been a deliberate strategy on the part of the government to cede its protections of this industry. Whether the industry can withstand the withering competition from abroad is still an open question, but it seems almost inevitable that Chinese companies will become even more reliant on their foreign partners for advanced technologies and management expertise once confronted with foreign competitors, unless a major effort is made by Chinese firms to improve their technological capabilities. Thus it appears that the Chinese government may again have reversed course with respect to its industrial policy.

At the same time, the Chinese government's 10th Five-Year Plan (2001–2005) for the automobile industry somewhat feebly tried to assert some independence from the world market. The plan stated that the guiding principles for the development of the automotive industry would be to persist in opening to the outside world while "boosting independent development capabilities"; to step up the "readjustment and upgrading of the product mix" with the parts-and-components sector as the foundation and economy cars as the priority; to optimize the organizational structure of the industry and achieve economies of scale; to accelerate the creation of a state-level technical center for strengthening Chinese technological innovation capacity and product development; to improve the market environment, reinforce legislation, and promote fair competition; and to sharpen the "competitive edge" of China's industry (Asia Pulse 2001).

The 2004 Auto Industry Policy

In May 2004, the Chinese National Development and Reform Commission issued its ten-year update to the 1994 Auto Industry Development Policy. For the first time, the government noted the emerging contradictions between the development of the auto industry and the encouragement of auto consumption by individual consumers on the one hand, and urban traffic infrastructure and environmental protection on the other hand. To resolve these contradictions, the policy states that the industry shall actively conduct research on electric and hybrid-electric vehicles, and that the state shall take measures in the areas of scientific research, technological innovation, industrialization of new technologies, and the creation of an enabling policy environment for the production and use of hybrid vehicles. The government also set a goal of reducing average fuel consumption by passenger vehicles by 15 percent by 2010 (CATARC 2004b).

With respect to technological innovation and capacity building, the policy states that the industry should continue to abide by the principle of integrating imported technologies with self-developed technologies, and that the state will support R&D activities through preferential tax policies. Article 3 of the policy is centered on motivating vehicle producers to boost their capabilities in R&D and technological innovation (CATARC 2004b).

The other major emphasis in the 2004 policy is continued industry restructuring. The objective stated is that automotive enterprises will grow into large-sized conglomerates, industrial alliances, and special-purpose vehicle producers to make the Chinese industry more competitive in the world market. For the first time, foreign investors will be allowed to control stakes of more than 50 percent in automobile and motorcycle joint ventures with Chinese partners *if* the joint ventures are built in China's export-processing zones and shoot at overseas markets (Xinhua Economic News Service 2005c).

Conclusion

This brief history reveals that Chinese government's automobile industry policy has flip-flopped several times since World War II, and that its policy signals aimed at foreign investors have been inconsistent. Initially, the government sought technology and training from the Soviet Union to create a foundation for China's own automobile industry. Because of the Sino-Soviet split, the government sealed itself away from the influence of foreign technology for two crucial decades when the U.S. and Japanese auto industries were innovating and realizing tremendous growth in production. During this period of isolation, the Chinese government fragmented the industry geographically, and eventually passenger-car production actually ceased.

After opening to the world in the 1970s, the industry was reborn, starting from essentially nothing except what remained of the old 1960s Soviet technology. No formal plan or set of policies for the auto industry was issued except to use any means possible to acquire more advanced technology. The government-owned auto firms both licensed technology from the Japanese and negotiated joint ventures with U.S. and European auto companies during that time. After several major joint ventures had been entered into, the Chinese government apparently reconsidered this strategy because it wanted to cultivate indigenous technological capabilities so that Chinese companies could compete in the world market. This new approach was enshrined in the 1994 Auto Industry Policy, and it resulted in the Chinese government's erecting even higher trade protections for its industry and making more stringent demands of foreign investors with respect to technology transfer. In a final reversal of policy, China decided to enter the WTO. The terms of China's entry mean that almost all of the requirements placed on foreign investors in 1994 must be lifted, and trade protections must be dismantled, all of which amounts to yet another complete turnaround of Chinese policy for the auto industry.

Such inconsistency has hindered the development of the Chinese auto industry. In Japan and Korea, government played a strong role in developing the auto industries through consistent protections, subsidies, and performance policies (Amsden 2001).[3] After the opening in China, the government seemed unable to decide whether it really wanted to have its own industry or whether it would be content to import vehicles as it had done early in the twentieth century. Once the government realized that the weak requirements it had held the foreigners accountable to had led the Chinese industry to become mere assemblers, it issued a landmark policy that finally imposed real technology-transfer requirements on the foreign investors. Yet this policy only endured for about five years because as China negotiated its entry into the WTO, it promised to remove all of these requirements as a price of entry.

It is somewhat ironic that the first period of rapid expansion in automobile production in China during the late 1990s coincided with the policy of more stringent technological requirements on foreigners. Now that these requirements are being eliminated, China's industry is scrambling to become more competitive. It is quite possible that China's auto industry will be again limited to automotive assembly due to its comparative advantage in low-cost labor. Without aggressive innovation on the part of the Chinese auto companies, they will be unlikely to be able to challenge the foreign companies. On the other hand, the increased competition inside the Chinese market had already contributed to considerable modernization of automotive technology during the late 1990s as producers scrambled to put more attractive products on the market.

The next three case studies will show how Chinese government policies strongly affected the nature of the Sino-U.S. joint ventures, the degree to which technology and knowledge were transferred within the joint ventures, and the factors contributing to their ultimate success or failure. Each case begins with a brief history, is followed by a section on technology transfer in the joint venture, and concludes with a discussion.

5

Beijing Jeep

Top executives in big companies only see China as a market to sell automobiles. They don't see China as a place to develop automobiles.
—Chinese employee of Beijing Jeep

China's First Experiment with a Foreign Joint Venture

Beijing Jeep Corporation (BJC) was the original trailblazer for Sino-foreign automobile joint ventures in China (see figure 5.1). In fact, it was the very first Chinese manufacturing joint venture signed with any foreign company after China reopened to the West in the late 1970s. The pioneering spirit once associated with Beijing Jeep flagged during the 1990s, and the joint venture continues to be troubled even though DaimlerChrysler AG signed a new thirty-year contract agreement with Beijing Automotive Industry Holding Company Ltd. (BAIC) in September 2003. This chapter evaluates technology transfer within Beijing Jeep from 1984 to 2002.

The U.S. firm that originally initiated the Beijing Jeep joint venture was not Chrysler, but American Motors Corporation (AMC). AMC was the owner of the Jeep sport-utility (SUV) brand, and it was also the last independent U.S. original-equipment manufacturer to be absorbed by the Big Three automakers. During the early 1980s AMC was struggling financially, so gaining access to the Chinese market was viewed as a coup unrivaled by any other U.S. automobile firm. Not only did AMC beat its own U.S. competitors to be the first company in the Chinese market, but AMC also beat out all the Japanese competitors as well. AMC's investment in China came at a time when U.S. companies were perceived

Figure 5.1
The gate of Beijing Jeep in downtown Beijing (photo by author)

to be losing out to the Japanese auto manufacturers. To illustrate how optimistic Wall Street was about the Chinese market, AMC's stock jumped 40 percent just after the announcement of the joint venture was leaked to the press in 1983 (Mann 1989). Yet the euphoria surrounding the investment failed to acknowledge some of the huge challenges that this new joint-venture company would face.

American Motors Corporation was founded in 1954 by a final consolidation of several of the smaller independent car companies, including Nash-Kelvinator Corporation and Hudson Motor Car Company.[1] In 1979 French car company Renault bought a minority stake of AMC with an agreement that AMC would sell Renault models in the United States. Almost a decade later, in 1987, Renault sold its stake to Chrysler. Chrysler eventually merged with Daimler-Benz to become Daimler-Chrysler AG in 1999. Each successive foreign owner assumed ownership of the minority foreign stake in Beijing Jeep. DaimlerChrysler's ancestors date back about a century to 1883, when Benz & Company was formed, and 1908, when Walter P. Chrysler produced his first automobile. Headquartered in Stuttgart, Germany, DaimlerChrysler currently owns a number of automotive brands including Chrysler, Dodge, Jeep, Mercedes-Benz, Maybach, Smart, AAV, a 37.3 percent stake in Mitsubishi Motors Corporation of Japan, and a 10 percent stake in Hyundai Motors of Korea. As of 2005, DaimlerChrysler AG had 181,241 employees with annual sales of US$64 billion (*Standard & Poor's Register of Corporations* 2005a). Aside from its automotive interests, Daimler-Chrysler is also currently in the aircraft, navigation, semiconductor, plastics, rubber, space, and missile businesses.

The Chinese partner has remained virtually unchanged throughout the twenty-year history of the joint venture. At the beginning, Beijing Automotive Works (BAW) was the owner of the Chinese share. BAW was a subsidiary of Beijing Automotive Industry Holding Corporation (BAIC), and the Beijing Municipality owned BAIC. A reorganization of the businesses resulted in the creation of a new firm called the Beijing Automotive Industry Holding Company Ltd. (BAIHC), which has taken over BAIC's role. Thus, the Chinese partner was, and still is, a state-owned enterprise.

Beijing Jeep is literally located in the heart of downtown Beijing, although a new factory is being built elsewhere. It is a five-minute taxi ride from the China World Trade Center and only a slightly longer distance from Zhongnanhai, the compound in central Beijing where many of the top Chinese leaders live and work. Such close proximity has assured the joint venture of special scrutiny, but at times the high visibility of this company has also played to BJC's advantage because no government leader, thus far, has been willing to let the first symbol of China's modernization and cooperation with the West completely perish. This situation has resulted in a paradox for Beijing Jeep. It continues to be strangled by its conservative state ownership, yet is kept alive by Beijing's reluctance to let it fail.

The motivation for the joint venture was compelling for both companies back in the late 1970s. At the time, the Chinese were producing the BJ212 (later the BJ2020), the technology of which was donated to China by the Soviets in the 1950s and transferred to Beijing Auto Works after the Cultural Revolution. This World War II–era utility vehicle was dated and ill-suited for the Chinese military's needs. In the early 1980s, the military was eager to obtain modern, soft-top, four-wheel-drive vehicles especially designed to meet Chinese specifications. In addition, the Chinese government wanted to modernize China's automobile industry. Since its own companies were so far behind world levels in terms of technological capability, the government felt that it had to turn to foreigners to acquire modern technology. The government hoped that the Chinese companies would learn from their foreign partners and acquire enough capabilities to produce a 100 percent Chinese-made all-terrain vehicle.

As it entered into negotiations with BAW, American Motors Corporation was in financial trouble at home. It was on the verge of collapse in 1979 when Renault, France's state-owned automaker, bought a 46 percent stake in the company. Almost ten years later, in 1987, Chrysler bought Renault's stake for US$1.1 billion in cash and Chrysler stock. Although AMC had only cost US$200 million in cash, it became a heavy burden for Chrysler because Chrysler had assumed about US$700 million in debt and approximately US$300 million worth of unfunded pension liabilities (Ingrassia and White 1994).

When AMC began negotiations in 1979, it was losing market share in the United States, in part because its gas-guzzling Jeeps were undesirable for consumers who were suddenly interested in fuel economy after the two oil shocks of the 1970s. The entire U.S. industry, in fact, was discovering that it lacked products that were competitive with the small, fuel-efficient Japanese cars. With a certain amount of hubris, it never seemed to occur to AMC that it might create a competitor by transferring technologies to a Chinese firm. The Japanese were more hardnosed. In fact, Toyota entered into negotiations with Beijing Auto Works, but was unwilling to actually transfer the technology to manufacture automobiles in China; Toyota was only interested in exporting automobiles directly to the Chinese mainland. In contrast, American Motors Corporation saw the potential of a vast market, incredibly low labor costs, and a potential export base for East Asia (Halberstam 1986; Mann 1989). Of course, American Motors Corporation was not the first U.S. firm to fall prey to the alluring idea of a boundless, untapped market for U.S. goods in China. This misconception dates back at least two centuries. As early as the nineteenth century, historian John Curtis Perry (1994, xix) notes, "[Americans] were, at least in a commercial sense, prepared to accept the Chinese myth that China, the Middle Kingdom, formed the center of the world. Americans believed that to command the trade of the Orient, potentially the world's most lucrative commerce, would be to capture global economic primacy."

Jim Mann (1989) identified three misleading myths that were accepted by AMC during its joint-venture negotiations with the Chinese: (1) since there were a billion people in China, there must be a large market, (2) foreign companies should establish a presence there, and (3) firms should be prepared to stay there for the long term. According to Mann, these assumptions were wrong because even though China had a billion people, almost none of them could afford to buy a car, not to mention that they did not want to buy a four-wheel-drive Jeep even if they had the money. Also, as time wore on, simply having a presence in the market did not automatically curry favor with the Chinese government, which was intent on winning the best terms that could be negotiated from any firm. The foreign companies failed to realize that the primary Chinese interests were to modernize their industry, and to protect it from too much competition while doing so. Last, most foreign firms that entered the Chinese automobile market seriously underestimated how long they would have to invest money there without earning any substantial returns.

On May 5, 1983, AMC accepted a minority stake in the joint venture for a term of twenty years. Of the total US$51 million in equity, Beijing provided US$35 million (mostly in equipment assets worth 69 percent), and AMC provided US$16 million (half of which was the contribution of technology). There were to be seven Chinese to four Americans on the board, and a Chinese executive would become board chair. For the first three years, an AMC representative would serve as president and CEO, and then the job would alternate between appointees of the Chinese and U.S. companies (Mann 1989). The plan was to continue production of the BJ212s for the first five years to keep a revenue stream going, to introduce AMC's Jeep Cherokee XJ model, and to develop the canvas-top military vehicle explicitly designed for China (to be introduced at some future date). The Cherokees were to be initially assembled from complete knockdown (CKD) kits that would be imported from the United States. It was agreed in a memorandum that the parts for the Cherokee would be gradually localized—that is, made by Chinese suppliers (Harwit 1995). An internal technology center was established (see figure 5.2), staffed almost entirely by Chinese engineers. As of 2002, there were approximately 200 Chinese engineers and only one foreign engineer employed there.

Figure 5.2
The technology center for Chinese engineers at Beijing Jeep (photo by author)

A major point of contention during the negotiations was how AMC would develop the new all-terrain vehicle with a soft canvas top. Although the contract called for development of the new model, it was short on specifics. The Chinese had yielded to AMC's insistence that this model would take millions of dollars, as well as years of design work, and agreed to accept the Cherokee as a stopgap vehicle for the interim period (Harwit 1995). The problem with this concession was that it provided few incentives for AMC to design a new vehicle. Indeed AMC's profit incentive was to simply sell as many kits of the Cherokee as possible to Beijing Jeep for assembly. The saving grace, if there was one, was that AMC still had an incentive to localize parts to save money on shipping the parts. After further exploration of the idea, AMC estimated it would take between US$700 million and US$1 billion to develop a new all-terrain vehicle for China. Since the entire joint venture was only worth US$51 million, AMC privately concluded that designing and developing a new vehicle was completely out of the question (Mann 1989).

Production and sales got off to a rocky start, and the entire joint venture almost crashed to a halt in 1986 when Beijing Jeep was unable to obtain enough foreign currency to purchase the Cherokee CKD kits from Detroit. The contract had specified that Beijing Jeep would earn foreign exchange by exporting its products, but the Beijing Jeep products were uncompetitive in quality and price on the world market, so no Jeeps had been exported. The Chinese government had established a policy that limited how much currency could be converted. After intervention by future Premier Zhu Rongji, the Chinese government eventually struck a secret deal in 1986 with Beijing Jeep alone to establish a special US$120 million fund to supply the necessary foreign exchange because it feared its model joint venture would fail. Once it recovered from this crisis, Beijing Jeep's production and sales of both the old BJ2020 and the Cherokee rose to a combined peak of 81,000 in 1995. After 1995, sales and production declined precipitously, falling to a rock-bottom low of 9,052 in 2002, a level lower than the number of vehicles produced at Beijing Auto Works before AMC entered the picture in 1983 (CATARC 2003). During this time (and through 2002) sales of the vintage BJ2020 consistently exceeded sales of the much newer Cherokee. The soft-top military vehicle desired by the Chinese was never designed or produced, although hundreds of Chinese engineers employed by Beijing Jeep persist in plodding along, trying to solve this vexing problem without foreign assistance.

A number of explanations exist for the astonishing decline of Beijing Jeep's production levels during the late 1990s. The most persuasive is that the original twenty-year contract was ending in 2003, and it seemed unlikely at the time that Chrysler was going to renew the contract. After all, Chrysler closed its Beijing office in 1997, saying that China's sluggish automobile market offered few opportunities for new projects (Bloomberg News 1997). That same year, BJC posted a 53 percent decline in sales from 1996 ("Losses at Venture in China" 1998). Aside from Beijing Jeep, Chrysler's only other international operations were located in Canada. Chrysler was unhappy with the joint venture in China, and it was perfectly content to let the old AMC contract that it had not negotiated expire. Once Daimler-Benz AG merged with Chrysler, it became clear that DaimlerChrysler had a completely different attitude. In contrast to Chrysler, the German company was international in its orientation, and had been trying to break into the Chinese market for some time. Aside from some involvements producing small numbers of trucks and buses in China, in 1995 Mercedes-Benz AG agreed to invest US$1 billion in a joint venture with Nanfang South China Motor Corporation to produce minivans, a car concept invented by Chrysler ("China's Car Industry: Ich Bin Ein Beijinger" 1995).[2]

Once Daimler-Benz and Chrysler merged in 1999, prospects for Beijing Jeep perked up. DaimlerChrysler immediately dispelled all the rumors that the company was going to pull out of China. It insisted that the Chinese market mattered to DaimlerChrysler and that the company was determined to commit to China. DaimlerChrysler quickly entered into contract negotiations with BAIC, and announced a new thirty-year contract in September 2003. Ownership under the contract is 42.4 percent held by DaimlerChrysler AG and 57.6 percent held by BAIC. The new joint venture is called Beijing-Benz-DaimlerChrysler Automotive Ltd. (BBDCA). Beijing Jeep had 3,800 employees in 2002. (DaimlerChrysler 2002).

At the end of 2002, Beijing Jeep announced that, in addition to the old products, it would also produce the Mitsubishi Challenger Pajaro Sport (otherwise known as the Montero) at the Beijing plant beginning in 2003.[3] In 2001, Beijing Jeep had introduced the Grand Cherokee, a luxury SUV, so the Pajaro fits into the SUV product portfolio above the Cherokee (later revamped as the Jeep 2500) and below the Grand Cherokee. Mitsubishi already has four models in production in China. It has arrangements with the South East (Fujian) Motor Corporation Ltd., Dongfeng Liuzhou Motor Company Ltd., and Harbin Hafei Motor Company Ltd. to assemble the Freeca, L300 Delica, Delica Space Gear, and Mirage Dingo models (Mitsubishi Motors Corporation 2002). In 2004, Beijing Jeep introduced the Mitsubishi Outlander as well.

Beijing Jeep never succeeded in securing permission from the government to produce regular sedan-sized passenger cars until 2004. This explicit goal for DaimlerChrysler was indirectly realized in late 2002 when a new joint venture between Beijing Automotive Industry Holding Company (BAIHC) and Korean Hyundai Motor Company was announced to produce sedans (initially the Hyundai Sonata). The total investment as of 2003 was be US$400 million with equal ownership. Hyundai became a "strategic partner" with DaimlerChrysler in 2000, meaning that DaimlerChrysler owns 10.46 percent of Hyundai.[4] Hyundai was established in 1967 in Korea, and it has grown into the eighth-largest automaker in the world (Hyundai Motor Corporation 2002). As of 2004, Beijing Hyundai sales had surged to 144,000 per year (Xinhua Financial Network News 2005c). In 2003, Beijing Jeep was renamed Beijing-Benz-DaimlerChrysler Automotive Ltd., and both firms now hold a 50 percent stake in the company. This new firm is allowed to produce a small number of Mercedes-Benz sedans in addition to the SUVs in a separate plant (Asia Pulse 2004).

Trial-and-Error Technology Transfer through the 1990s

Before 2001, the bulk of the technology transfer in Beijing Jeep occurred just after AMC and BAW launched their joint venture in the mid-1980s. From the start, both sides agreed to produce BAW's existing BJ212 (which was renamed the BJ2020) for five years while the Cherokee was introduced. As it turned out, the old BJ212 proved to be quite profitable for Beijing Jeep. The technology might have been of 1950s vintage, but it continued to sell fairly well, especially to the Chinese military, which bought several thousand per year (see figure 5.3). Later, the engine and some other components from the Cherokee were adapted for the BJ2020, although it outwardly remained essentially the same in appearance (interview with E. Clark, director, Product Engineering, Beijing Jeep Corporation, Beijing, 2002). The Americans continued to support selling it even though they had no responsibility for the technology, while Beijing Jeep could reap the profits, convert them into dollars, and purchase kits from Detroit for the Cherokees. As Mann (1989, 228) notes, "It was the ultimate irony: An American corporation that originally expected to reap huge profits by bringing modern technology to China and by selling its superior products to the Chinese found itself surviving, indeed thriving, by selling the Chinese old Chinese products."

Somewhat surprisingly, in interviews with the Chinese technical engineers employed at the BJC Technical Center, they staunchly supported

Figure 5.3
The BJ2020 incarnation of the old BJ212 model (left) and the Cherokee (right) produced by Beijing Jeep (photo by author)

the old BJ2020, considering it to be "their" model. The BJ2020 is the only model that they have ever been allowed to tinker with (and learn from), and they felt that its existence justifies their *own* existence (interview with Beijing Jeep Chinese employees 2002).

AMC introduced its Cherokee Jeep XJ—which had recently been launched in the United States and was proving to be quite popular there—to China in 1984. At the time, the Cherokee produced in China was identical to the U.S. version (interview with E. Clark, Beijing, 2002). Initially, Beijing Jeep purchased Cherokee kits from AMC and then assembled those kits at Beijing Jeep for subsequent sale in China. AMC did not really make any money from selling the vehicles in China, profiting instead from the sale of the kits to BJC. This structure reduced the incentive for AMC to transfer any knowledge about the technology.

The Chinese government soon realized that there were two major problems with this arrangement. First, the purchase of the kits was a drain on China's foreign currency because the kits had to be bought with U.S. dollars, and BJC was not earning any foreign exchange since it could not export due to the high cost and poor quality of the automobiles. The technology transfer was also limited because the Chinese workers did not have to learn anything except how to assemble the parts sent to them.

In response, the Chinese government issued a policy that BJC would not have to apply for import licenses for the CKD parts if the automobiles contained less than 40 percent local content. This incentive spurred AMC to work with local suppliers to bring the quality of the Chinese-made products up to an acceptable standard. By 1993, Beijing Jeep had achieved 61 percent localization for the Cherokee parts and components (Harwit 1995). Thus, one could argue that the main technological contribution of AMC's Cherokee was not the Cherokee technology itself, but its resulting backward linkages into China's parts-and-components industry. In the end, Beijing Jeep eventually did manage to localize most of the parts and components for the Cherokee, and as of 2002, more than 90 percent of all Cherokee parts were made by suppliers in China (interview with W.-M. Soh, vice president, Special Projects, BJC Sales and Marketing, DaimlerChrysler, Beijing, 2002). In the new 2002 contract with DaimlerChrysler, the Chinese were granted full rights to the Cherokee, which is no longer produced in the United States or anywhere else in the world.

The Cherokee technology was not always updated or refreshed in tandem with updates to U.S. models after being introduced to China in 1984. The original engine dated back to 1968, although it was updated significantly over time. Some of the functional changes made in the United States were maintained in China, such as the electronic fuel-injection engine, brake improvements, and distributorless ignitions. But other updates were not made. For example, in 1997, the U.S. Cherokee had a major refreshing, but some of the 1997 updates were not made in China, such as the new body sheet metal, new interior, new fenders, and new grille (interview with E. Clark, Beijing, 2002).

Beijing Jeep officials offer several reasons for the stagnation of the technology in China until the late 1990s. First, if a component or system had been localized in China (a Chinese firm was supplying the part), sometimes the old version was maintained in China only, as in the case of the 1997 Cherokee updates that were not transferred to China. Second, if production volume was too low, it was nearly impossible to recover the capital costs of retooling the equipment and introducing new designs. One official said that a million automobiles must be produced before the investment in the tooling is paid off, so at their late-1990s production rate of less than 10,000 automobiles per year, it would take more than a century to be able to recover their capital investment and retool. Third, since no other similar autos in the Chinese market were really competing with BJC until the late 1990s, there was little incentive to introduce newer technologies.

Aside from the lack of competition in this market segment, the last explanation proffered by a Beijing Jeep official for the dated vintage of the technologies was that since the Chinese government did not want to hurt the Chinese firms that do not have joint ventures with foreign firms (especially the smaller ones), it has been slow to require changes in the industry as a whole. One U.S. employee commented that technical change was driven by government policies in the United States, so if the Chinese government put policies in place to require the use of advanced technologies, the companies would somehow find a way to do it, and the foreign companies would "certainly" transfer the necessary technologies. The fact that sales were dropping off so steeply at Beijing Jeep only worsened the dilemma because less and less money was available for investment (interview with E. Clark, Beijing, 2002).

Despite the enormous dissatisfaction on the Chinese side that they still have not obtained a new soft-top all-terrain vehicle, it does not appear that much has changed since the introduction of the Cherokee. For fifteen years, Beijing Jeep essentially manufactured the same Cherokee model (albeit with some updates) and the old BJ2020 (with the updates from the Cherokee) year after year. Finally in 1998, Beijing Jeep introduced a long-wheelbase (LWB) Cherokee to the market because it added more features and comfortable legroom for passengers in the back seat to accommodate the Chinese consumers who hire drivers and ride in the back. In 2001, Chrysler introduced a new model, the luxurious Grand Cherokee, the first new model in seventeen years (Treece 2002a). In May 2003, Beijing Jeep introduced a new Cherokee model to replace the old Cherokee called the Jeep 2500. The interior, exterior, and major systems (such as the four-wheel disk brakes and transmission) were all updated and are "up to current worldwide automotive standards" (interview with E. Clark, Beijing, 2002).

In terms of the energy and environmental performance of Beijing Jeep's products, DaimlerChrysler is below average due to the relatively poor fuel efficiency of the models. In 2000, when EURO I standards took effect, the Chinese government required all new cars to be installed with electronic fuel-injection devices and catalytic converters. Zhu Yunde, general manager of Beijing Jeep at the time emission standards were issued, estimated that meeting the new standards for the BJ2020 and certain Cherokee 7250 models would cause sales of those models to drop by 15 percent until the company could bring those models into compliance (China Business Information Network 1998b). But as of 2003, all of Beijing Jeep's models met the EURO II standards required in the cities, and the Jeep Grand Cherokee purportedly meets EURO III standards, according to Beijing Jeep sources. In terms of fuel efficiency, the various Jeep models get 14–21 miles per gallon.

Lack of Modernization

Although Beijing Jeep is the longest-standing automobile joint venture in China, Chinese engineers employed at the company still feel they have not been able to acquire any advanced technological capabilities. One Chinese engineer working there lamented, "I'm not even sure that we are even where Chrysler was in 1980," adding that "the only way to close the gap is for DaimlerChrysler to send engineers to China to work with us." When the company was healthier financially, Chrysler sent some Chinese engineers to Detroit for training, but there has been no exchange like this since the mid-1990s. Even then, the training was "piecemeal and short," according to one trainee. The Chinese would be shown around and then given easy things to do, isolated from the rest of the company. To really learn, in this trainee's opinion, the Chinese should be sent for a longer time and allowed to work in every division so they can learn about what each part of the company does and how the divisions work together as a team (interview with a Beijing Jeep Chinese employee 2002).

A long-standing frustration for the Chinese engineers is that the U.S. side has never permitted any deviation from the precise specifications provided for the Cherokee. The positive aspect of this rule is that they learned a lot by working with the parts suppliers to get specifications met, but since Chrysler has been so inflexible, no creativity or innovation on the part of the Chinese engineers has ever been encouraged or rewarded. A high-ranking Chinese engineer at Beijing Jeep commented, "The top executives in the big companies only see China as a market to sell automobiles. They don't see China as a place to *develop* automobiles" (interview with a Beijing Jeep Chinese employee 2002). Indeed, the vice president for Special Projects, BJC Sales and Marketing, at DaimlerChrysler China asserted, "We are here to make money—that means with the proper business model in making the joint venture profitable—and in the meantime perform respective training" (interview with W.-M. Soh, Beijing, 2002).

In Beijing Jeep, technology transfer works primarily through the localization process. DaimlerChrysler will provide specifications to Beijing Jeep for new products, and it is Beijing Jeep's job to try to localize them. The Chinese engineers study the specifications at their technical center until they think they fully understand them, and then the engineers go to a supplier to make sure the supplier understands the specifications perfectly. Eventually the supplier tries to make the part and usually runs into all kinds of problems. First, it might realize that it has the wrong tools or equipment, or maybe it does not have the right materials, or it discovers that it simply does not know how to produce the part. So then the BJC engineers have to go back to DaimlerChrysler to figure out what they are doing wrong. In the end, the BJC engineers learn a lot through this "learning-by-doing" process, but it is slow, frustrating, and costly (interview with a Beijing Jeep Chinese employee 2002). Thus, knowledge about how to produce the Cherokee parts to specification is being transferred from DaimlerChrysler to BAW, but how to put the parts together (or design new interrelated parts) appears to still be beyond the reach of the Chinese engineers at Beijing Jeep.

Chinese engineers at Beijing Jeep's Technology Center have repeatedly tried to develop their "100 percent Chinese-made" vehicle. In a recent attempt, they assembled a concept car called the *Heroic*, so named because they wanted to display it at the Beijing Auto Show in 2000 and had chosen the name to represent the pride of the team that designed it. In Chinese, they call it the *Beijing Er* (second generation), because it was their second try at developing a new vehicle (interview with a Beijing Jeep Chinese employee 2002). The *Beijing Er* had a new body, but essentially used many Cherokee technologies under the hood. The vehicle design was completed, but it was canceled due to the lack of financial feasibility (interview with E. Clark, Beijing, 2002). In 2002, the BJC Technology Center engineers displayed their latest concept car: the *Yong Shi* (brave soldier), which is, not surprisingly, a soft-top jeep geared for military use.

To visit the Jeep factory, one must negotiate the downtown streets of Beijing, which are teeming with people, taxis, bicycles, vendors, and trucks. On arrival, one expects to find just as much activity on the inside of the gate as on the outside. Yet, when observed on two separate visits during the summer of 2002, the entire factory was at a standstill. Workers were nowhere to be seen, the cluster of buildings was eerily silent, and two visitors were able to cross the entire campus without encountering a single person aside from a solitary street sweeper. Entering the stamping factory was especially shocking because the gigantic machines were poised motionless, bereft of any workers even doing maintenance on them during this downtime. When inquiring why the factories were still, visitors could only extract vague explanations about "supply-and-demand" problems. If this was a sign of the times, prospects indeed seem grim for Beijing Jeep. Still, Tong Zhiyuan, executive vice president of the company, announced in June 2003 that it was beginning to earn a slight profit for the first time in years because it cut nearly 5,000 employees (SinoCast 2003). In 2004, sales continued to grow, reaching 32,000 vehicles.

6

Shanghai GM

We did everything we promised to do.
—Philip Murtaugh, former chair and CEO of GM China

The foreign companies are not good teachers, but the Chinese companies are not so clever.
—Chinese national working for GM China

The Risk Takers

General Motors' Corp. (GM) influence in China dates back nearly as long as the company has been in existence. In 1922, GM cars began to be exported to China, and by the 1930s one out of every six vehicles on China's roads had a Buick nameplate. Most of these cars were motoring around Shanghai, a city more accustomed to foreign influences than most in China because of its status as a treaty port during the late Qing Dynasty (1644–1911). Thus in 1999, when Buick sedans started rolling off production lines at the Shanghai General Motors Co. Ltd. (Shanghai GM) plant in Pudong, the older Shanghainese were already familiar with the Buick name (see figure 6.1). This chapter assesses technology transfer at Shanghai GM between 1998 and 2002.

Of the U.S. Big Three automakers, only GM had secured a solid foothold in China as of 2005. This achievement can best be explained by the GM leadership's high-risk, aggressive approach and strong public commitment to manufacturing automobiles in China, which attracted the Chinese government's support. When GM first entered the Chinese market, it brought the most modern technology to date of any foreign investor, it established one of the best working relationships of any

Figure 6.1
The gate to Shanghai GM (photo by author)

Sino-foreign joint venture with its Chinese partner, Shanghai Automotive Industry Corporation (SAIC), and GM set new standards of technology transfer that other foreign companies scrambled to match due to the increasing competitiveness of the market. As of 2004, Shanghai GM was the third-largest passenger-car producer in China, selling 252,109 units that year (Xinhua Financial Network News 2005b).

General Motors, the largest automobile company in the world, is headquartered in Detroit, Michigan. It also is the world's largest company in terms of revenue and number of employees—in 2005, GM had 326,000 employees and annual sales of US$193 billion (*Standard & Poor's Register of Corporations* 2005c). Aside from its automobile-related businesses, GM is also a producer of electronics, locomotives, and space products.

SAIC is known as China's top passenger-car producer. In 2004, it sold 843,000 vehicles, with a net profit of 1.98 billion yuan (Xinhua Financial Network News 2005a).[1] SAIC formed its first joint venture with a foreign company in 1984, when it joined forces with Volkswagen. SAIC had 60,000 employees and a total sales revenue of 98 billion RMB (US$11 billion) in 2001 (SAIC 2003).

There was some ambivalence within GM in the early years about whether there would be a sufficiently big market, developing fast enough, in China to warrant a significant investment there. At one international policy-committee meeting, a Chinese employee at GM did a presentation on what it would take to produce cars in China. The then CEO reportedly asked the man how many cars he expected to produce in the first few years. The analyst replied, "After several years, about 20,000–30,000 cars." The CEO replied that the estimated level was not interesting, and that was the end of the meeting (interview with R. Frosch, Cambridge, MA, 2002). This estimate, by the way, is exactly how many cars Shanghai GM did produce in its first two years.

But GM's chair John Smith apparently had a different attitude toward China during the 1990s. At the signing ceremony for Shanghai GM, Smith declared, "This project is a critical element in GM's total network" (Bloomberg News 1997). As a result, GM's commitment to China was strong throughout the 1990s, and capable executives led GM's effort in China at the time.

Once GM decided to get into the Chinese market, it did so with vigor. Other foreign manufacturers—including American Motors Corporation (taken over by Chrysler) and Volkswagen—had been in the marketplace for ten or more years before GM signed its passenger-car joint-venture contract with SAIC in 1997. In 1994, GM opened a China office in Beijing, and in 1995, GM began negotiations for a major passenger-car joint venture. During his visit to China in 1997, Vice President Al Gore witnessed the signing of GM's US$1.52 billion deal to create Shanghai GM. It is often reported that GM's investment represents the largest single U.S. foreign direct investment in China (Faison 1998; GM 2001). GM and SAIC each contributed US$350 million in cash, and together they were responsible for $820 million in bank loans, of which GM was responsible for half in the event of a default (interview with P. Murtaugh, chair and CEO, China Group, General Motors China, Shanghai, 2002).

GM was anxious to win the joint venture with SAIC because it believed SAIC was the "best automobile company in China" (interview in Detroit with C. Green, executive director, Regional Science and Technology, General Motors Asia Pacific Ltd., 2002). Indeed, SAIC had many advantages, including that it was reputed to be the most profitable

Chinese automobile company and that it had been publicly chosen by the Chinese government to be the primary Chinese passenger-car producer. SAIC was also known to have a good sense of the passenger-car market—a reputation that was only enhanced by its location in Shanghai, where the locals are renowned for their business acumen and attention to detail. The one, potentially large, disadvantage was that SAIC was already involved in a major joint venture with Volkswagen called Shanghai VW (SVW). This joint venture produced the most passenger cars of any entity in China, and held 54 percent of the market share at that time (CATARC 2000).[2]

GM was quite attractive to the Chinese simply because it is the largest automobile company in the world. Matching this world powerhouse with China's leading passenger-car producer was undeniably appealing to the Chinese. Although many foreign companies bid on the joint venture with SAIC, GM's main competition was Ford Motor Company. Toyota bid on the SAIC project, but it dropped out due to an unwillingness to meet the technology-transfer requirements desired by the Chinese government. Germany's Volkswagen was already in alliance with SAIC, and the French firm, Citroën, had just signed a joint-venture contract with Dongfeng Automobile Company in 1992. In the end, GM China's Philip Murtaugh believes that GM won the partnership with SAIC because the Chinese company simply liked GM's products better, and that the joint venture could just as easily have gone to Ford (Murtaugh 2002).

Although Shanghai GM is GM's flagship operation in China, GM formed three other joint ventures across China during the 1990s and made a number of indirect investments as well. Two of the other joint ventures are for automotive manufacturing: Jinbei GM in Shenyang, Liaoning Province, and SAIC-GM-Wuling in Guangxi Province. Jinbei GM began operation in 1992, shut down from 1995 to 1998, and restarted its production of Chevy Blazers in 1998. Jinbei GM has floundered for two main reasons. First, the ownership of the Chinese partner firm has changed several times. Second, although Jinbei GM is only allowed to produce sport-utility vehicles (SUVs), urban Chinese consumers have simply been uninterested in SUVs as passenger cars, viewing them mainly as trucks for the rural areas. Even so, GM planned to introduce the Chevrolet Trailblazer and Tahoe SUV models in 2003 (Business Daily Update 2003). The SAIC-GM-Wuling joint venture was established in 2002, and it is GM's most recent and smallest investment in China. Wuling is one of the most prominent manufacturers of minibuses in China, so this investment widens GM's product portfolio.

During the joint-venture negotiations over Shanghai GM, the Chinese government insisted that GM had to establish a technical center with SAIC. This desire had been expressed to other foreign companies in the past, but GM was the first company to actually agree to create one. Therefore, GM established a separate US$50 million joint venture with SAIC called the Pan-Asia Technical Automotive Center (PATAC), with equity split equally between partners (see figure 6.2). The purpose of PATAC is to provide engineering support to Shanghai GM and other auto companies in China. Although PATAC is separate from Shanghai GM, most of its business comes from its sister joint venture. PATAC had

Figure 6.2
PATAC Technical Center joint venture: "Join the field of international automotive development and establish the promising future of the Chinese automotive industry" (photo by author)

400 engineers in 2002, and 80 percent of its work was done for Shanghai GM at that time (interview with GM China Chinese employee B, Shanghai, 2002).

It should be noted that GM also has some indirect investments in China. Aside from stakes in parts-and-components companies, GM's biggest indirect investment is through its 20 percent stake in Suzuki, which has a joint venture in Chongqing with Chang'An Automobile (Group) Corp. Chang'An also has a separate joint venture with Ford (see chapter 7). Finally, like other foreign firms, GM has tried to export autos to China with limited success. In December 2000, GM registered only its ten-thousandth-export sale to China.

For the opening day of production at Shanghai GM in December 1998, GM Chair Jack Smith flew to China and personally drove the first automobile—a Buick *Xin Shi Ji* (New Century) luxury sedan—off the production line (see figure 6.3).[3] The sedan was priced at about 330,000 RMB (US$40,000). At the time, there was little competition for luxury automobiles in the domestic market. There was the imported Audi 200, the old domestically produced Audi 100, and the Red Flag (*Hongqi*) sedan produced by First Auto Works that was lower than the Buick in

Figure 6.3
The Buick luxury sedan produced at Shanghai GM (photo by author)

price and not really a competitor. Once the luxury Buick entered the market, Audi responded with its Audi A6, which is priced above the Buick, and Honda began producing its Accord in Guangzhou at a slightly lower price of 280,000 RMB (US$34,000), eventually forcing SGM to lower its price to 280,000 RMB as well. Finally, VW introduced its Passat, which was priced directly against the Buick and the Honda Accord.

SGM started production of the *Xin Shi Ji* with 47 percent of the parts made by local Chinese suppliers, in accordance with the Chinese requirement of 40 percent local content. In 1997, Larry Zahner, president of GM China, predicted that SGM would buy US$1.6 billion dollars worth of parts and services from the United States during the next five years (China Business Information Network 1998a). In 1999, 20,000 Buick sedans were produced, and by 2000 SGM had localized 60 percent of the parts, importing only US$140 million worth of parts annually from the United States (Graham 2000). As of 2005, SGM was among the top three producers in China along with Shanghai VW and FAW-VW. The three companies combined accounted for 72 percent of sedan sales in 2004 (Xinhua Financial Network News 2005c).

Only two years after introducing its inaugural luxury sedan, which was targeted at government officials and the wealthy, Shanghai GM launched a compact sedan called the Buick Sail (*Sai Ou*). This car was targeted at private consumers in the burgeoning Chinese middle class (see figure 6.4). Priced at about 100,000 RMB (US$12,000) initially, this compact was put into the market against the VW Jetta and Tianjin Xiali (and also against the VW Santana, which is a bigger car but is sold at a similar price). The Sail was based on the Brazilian Chevrolet Corsa, which was based on the original German Opel Corsa, versions of which are sold in eighty countries around the world. It had dual air bags and antilock brakes as standard features, a first for a compact car in China (Leicester 2000). There were two versions of the Buick Sail: one was a compact sedan (see figure 6.4) and the other was a hatchback called the Sail-RV.

Although outside the scope of this book's analysis, Shanghai GM has continued to introduce more models and refine its offerings since 2002.

Figure 6.4
Buick Sail on display at Beijing Auto Show 2002 (photo by author)

Early in 2003, SGM introduced a new model, the Buick Excelle (based on a GM Daewoo platform), to compete directly against the SVW Santana (Agence France Presse 2003). SGM also produced a GL8 minivan, which was not a focus of this study. More recently, Shanghai GM greatly expanded its product offerings, launching ten new models in 2005 alone (SinoCast 2005).

As of 2003, Shanghai GM had risen to be the third-largest producer of passenger cars in China, behind Shanghai VW and First Auto Works–VW. In only four years, SGM captured 11 percent of the Chinese market, and the Shanghai GM factory in Pudong was producing at its maximum capacity. Sales of GM products grew 325 percent between 2001 and 2002 (Business Daily Update 2003). Because demand for SGM vehicles continued to be so strong, and because it needed additional production space, SGM bought a separate factory in Yantai, Shandong Province, in December 2002 in order to be able to double its production of Buick sedans (Fackler 2002). As of 2000, Shanghai GM had about 2,500 workers (Leicester 2000). The average employee earned about US$4,000 a year, four times the national average income (Graham 2000).

Raising the Bar for Technology Transfer

Since Shanghai GM's inception in 1997, all of its passenger-car models were transferred to China using the same technology-transfer process: GM developed the automotive technology and manufacturing design, and then transferred it to Shanghai GM for production. By internal accounts, the technology-transfer processes themselves have been very efficient and without major difficulties (interview with C. Green, Detroit, 2002). The product adaptation for the Chinese market was done entirely by GM for the luxury sedan, but for the Sail, PATAC and SGM did most of the product adaptation.

According to GM China CEO Murtaugh, the Buick luxury sedan being produced in China (see figure 6.3) is a completely different car than its equivalent produced for the United States. The Chinese New Century Buick was based on two models sold in the U.S. market: the Buick Century and Buick Regal. SGM made approximately 600 changes to these U.S. designs, seven of which were major, before and during the first three years of production of the luxury sedan. The engine was "designed new" for China by GM Powertrain. The engine in the United States had two options, a 3.1-liter V6 60° engine and a 3.8-liter 90° engine. GM took the 60° version and restroked it to 2.98 liters to meet Chinese government requirements that all government officials who are provided passenger cars must have a 3.0-liter engine or smaller. Because fuel economy turned out to be important to Chinese consumers, SGM later introduced a second engine with 2.5-liter displacement. The suspension was entirely new and the interior seats were redesigned for the Chinese body type. SGM put new door pads on, and upgraded the interior from gray cloth to tan leather. In addition, a sunroof was added and significant improvements were made in noise reduction (about US$70 of the price of each car is for noise reduction alone). In Murtaugh's opinion, the Chinese version has some better performance characteristics, better fuel economy, and better noise levels than the U.S. model (interview with P. Murtaugh, Shanghai, 2002).

Shanghai GM was the first Sino-foreign firm to make significant changes to a model once it was in production in China. Previously, the Sino-foreign joint ventures would just keep the same old model in production interminably until it seemed woefully outdated. Then a new model would be introduced for a higher price, but the old one would continue to be produced at a lower price. At the beginning in 1998, SGM produced three versions of the New Century luxury sedan: the GL, GLX, and XSJ. After six months, SGM released the GS, which had the new suspension system and also a new monotone exterior without chrome. In another six months, SGM put in the 2.5-liter engine, upgraded the interior to leather, and added the sunroof. Thus, the Chinese Buick in production today is quite different from the original version produced in 1998. The principal reason why SGM continued to introduce improved technologies was because of increased competition in the marketplace. SGM raised the bar by introducing a relatively modern automobile into the domestic market, but then paid the price when its competitors responded with similarly modern and attractive sedans (Honda Accord, Audi A6, and VW Passat). As Murtaugh noted, "SGM both had to improve its product *and* lower price a little because of increased competition. This will be true for other companies as well, and you can already see it in the Passat and Honda Accord" (interview with P. Murtaugh, Shanghai, 2002).

SGM launched the Buick Sail (see figure 6.4) in a great rush to meet the rising demand for more economical sedans. GM realized they had to choose a model that could be introduced to China quickly. According to Murtaugh, the most important consideration in choosing the model was speed to production, so this is the main reason why the Opel Corsa was picked. SGM did not want to lose market share to other firms like the Tianjin FAW Xiali Corporation Ltd., which was already introducing compact sedans such as the Xiali 2000, using Toyota Echo technology. The Corsa had already been introduced into developing-country markets such as Brazil, Mexico, and Spain, so the design work was, in Murtaugh's words, "90 percent done." At the time, the Corsa was manufactured at eight locations in the world—thus, it was not a new technology. Because the design work was mostly complete, it was both cheaper and faster to introduce the Corsa than any other GM model.

Even so, SGM had to modify the suspension, engine calibration (because of Chinese fuel quality), exterior styling, grille, headlamps, and side fascia. By this time, PATAC had acquired enough product-adaptation capabilities to do most of the modifications by itself. SGM started production of the Sail in 2001 with 70 percent local content, the highest level ever for a joint venture in China. This achievement was possible because SGM had already developed relationships with parts-and-components suppliers through the manufacture of the New Century, and also because Shanghai VW had cultivated local suppliers in Shanghai. These suppliers had learned to produce parts and components to the relatively high standards of the Sino-foreign joint ventures.

The Sail's competition originally was the Jetta, Citroën/Dongfeng Fukang, and Xiali 2000. Shortly after the Sail blew into the market, Shanghai VW responded by introducing its new Polo, apparently a version of the Golf, which seems to be more modern than Shanghai VW's Jetta or Santana, both of which are old designs.

In both of its automobile models, Shanghai GM introduced a more modern product than was being produced by Shanghai VW and by most of SGM's other competitors. And, in both cases, the competitors either upgraded their product or brought in an entirely new model in response to SGM's product. For example, Shanghai VW responded to the Buick luxury sedan with a new Passat, and SVW responded to the Sail with the Polo. Since GM has the same domestic partner as VW, one cannot help but wonder how loyal SAIC is to GM. According to Murtaugh, GM was originally worried about VW but by the end of 1997, this concern had become a "nonissue" because they had cultivated such a close working relationship and trust was high. Intellectual property rights have been "no real problem" according to Murtaugh, although there have been some "normal" amounts of leakage akin to what would be found between companies in the United States or Europe (interview with P. Murtaugh, Shanghai, 2002). It is clear that the threat of GM's products pushed VW to transfer better technology to SAIC and to upgrade SVW's production lines. This increased competition between SGM and SVW clearly is benefiting the Chinese consumer because better products, at lower prices, are being offered. Yet SAIC may have stronger loyalties to SGM than SVW because SAIC owns a bigger equity stake in SGM (50 percent) versus SVW (25 percent).

"Manufacturing Alone, Not Technology Development"

SAIC apparently drew lessons from its experience with Volkswagen to guide its joint-venture negotiations with GM. During the negotiations, both GM and SAIC agreed that the correct way to run the joint venture was to focus on the benefit of the joint venture itself, instead of mainly profiting from supplying parts to the joint venture. GM could have focused on selling complete knockdown (CKD) kits to the joint venture, and SAIC could similarly have focused on selling its own Chinese-made parts to the joint venture, but GM and SAIC agreed to make it a priority to reduce costs at the joint-venture level (interview with P. Murtaugh, Shanghai, 2002). Otherwise, like other foreign firms before it, GM might have been content to export CKD parts to the joint venture and earn money from the sales of the kits.

Similarly, GM appears to have learned from the experience of other foreign firms in China. From the start, GM displayed an aggressively committed and cooperative attitude toward China. A pyramid-shaped graphic containing GM's goals and principles in China was displayed at the signing of the SGM joint venture. At the top of the pyramid was the following vision: to grow the business to be among the top three in market share (achieved in 2002), to be number one in customer satisfaction, and to localize the management. The core values were customer enthusiasm, integrity, teamwork, innovation, and continuous improvement. With respect to principles, GM stated that it would actively engage in technology exchange and foster Chinese managerial and professional development, and that GM's partnership with China would be long-term and win-win (interview with C. Green, Detroit, 2002).

Murtaugh believes that the joint venture has been successful because GM and SAIC's goals are completely in alignment and because they have worked hard to make the relationship a good one. Each decision has been made with the goal of making the joint venture more successful. The good working relationship that emerged between Murtaugh and SAIC President Hu Maoyuan at the top levels was modeled at lower levels (Kraar 1999).[4] Asked why there appeared to be such a high level of trust between GM and SAIC, Murtaugh responded, "We did everything we promised to do."

In terms of technology transfer, few barriers within the actual process have emerged. From GM's point of view, the biggest problem with the technology-transfer process was how to measure it so that SAIC could be sure it was not getting cheated. SAIC was exceedingly worried based on its prior experience (and that of other Chinese companies) that GM would put hurdles in the way of technology transfer. The Chinese came up with a measurement scheme that classified technologies into a number of categories such as outline drawings, assembly drawings, detailed specifications, and so forth. Eventually, GM was able to convince SAIC that specifications and drawings simply did not exist for every aspect of production. Some of the technology, or knowledge, was just inside the heads of the engineers who work for GM. SAIC lacked the experience and knowledge to realize that much of the technology they were trying to acquire was tacit. Although the technology-transfer process contained few barriers, it was not without cost. The process is expensive, especially because of the need for engineering support from experts in the United States, and this is a key inhibitor to more advanced technology transfer (interview with GM China Chinese employee A, Beijing, 2002).

There is evidence that GM has indeed followed through on its promises to exchange technology and foster Chinese managerial and professional development. Still, as of 2002, the Chinese had not acquired significantly enhanced technological capabilities through their joint venture with GM; for example, SAIC still lacked design capabilities. This outcome is attributable to the simple lack of incentives for SAIC to be more motivated to acquire better capabilities and for GM to teach its partners anything beyond what is needed to get the models into production and manufacture them well. As one Chinese manager working for GM commented, "The foreign companies are not good teachers, but the Chinese companies are not so clever"(interview with GM China Chinese employee A, Beijing, 2002). This employee argued that in general, the Chinese automotive firms need to work on finding good teachers: "As a parent, you know that if your child stays home and tries to read and learn, she will make progress, but not as much as if she has a really good teacher, so you try to find her a good teacher and get her into that school." This Chinese employee said that if he were the boss of a Chinese company, he would try to find the best teachers internationally. Of course, the main purpose of the joint venture is to manufacture automobiles in China. He pointed out that the SGM joint venture is for *manufacturing* alone, not for *technology development* (his emphasis). The development of technology is clearly separate from Shanghai GM, and if SGM wants more advanced technology, it will come from GM but at a cost, because all new technology transfer is negotiated and paid for separately (interview with GM China Chinese employee A, Beijing, 2002). Outside of the SGM joint venture, GM does invest in applied research projects conducted by Chinese universities and institutes, and such projects support the development of Chinese capabilities in academia. From 1996 to 2002, GM invested nearly US$2 million in such projects (interview with C. Green, Detroit, 2002).

It must also be noted that SAIC has been slow to exert itself to enhance its own technological capabilities. Under significant pressure from the Chinese government, SAIC finally set up an R&D center of its own called the Automotive Engineering Academy of SAIC in August 2002, the first of its kind for a Chinese manufacturer. SAIC said that the center symbolized the beginning of China's efforts to develop automotive technology independently (CIIC 2002).

GM's environmental performance in China has been average. Like most other foreign joint ventures, SGM produced EURO II–compliant vehicles to meet the Chinese government's emission standards for the big cities.[5] These standards lagged behind U.S. standards by nearly a decade (see table 2.2), so it cannot be said that GM transferred best-available environmental technologies to China. GM has been somewhat more proactive than other foreign firms in working with the Chinese government to promote understanding about air-pollution control in vehicles (interview with an official from the China State Environmental Protection Administration (SEPA), Cambridge, NIA, 2002). For example, GM paid for a SEPA study on how to phase out leaded fuel, sponsored a workshop on onboard diagnostic technology, donated an electric car to the Ministry of Science and Technology (MOST)'s electric-vehicle demonstration project in Shantou, and helped to set up an emissions testing center at PATAC. In terms of fuel efficiency, the SGM cars are also average. Even so, GM deserves credit for introducing a more fuel-efficient model to meet consumer demand. But introduction of inefficient models like the Chevy Blazer and the Cadillac will worsen GM's overall fuel efficiency in China. The fuel efficiencies of the Chinese models seemed roughly comparable to their model counterparts in the United States or Europe as of 2004.

In summary, GM has been the most successful by far of all the U.S. investors in penetrating the Chinese market and in cultivating a reasonably good working relationship with its Chinese partner. GM did not try to cultivate its Chinese partner's technological capabilities beyond what was needed to make the manufacturing operation efficient and profitable, but it invested in a substantial number of applied research projects at Chinese universities and institutes. Its environmental performance was not remarkably good, but it was at least average through 2004.

7

Chang'An Ford

Ford should be more open technologically because there would be mutual benefit.
—Chinese Engineer at Chang'An Automobile (Group) Corp. Co.

The Risk Averse

As of 2004, Ford Motor Company had taken a more risk-averse approach to China than the other U.S. companies that have invested there. Of the Big Three, Ford was the last to manufacture a passenger car in China, and thus it has the weakest reputation there. Ford's involvement in China dates back to 1913, when a small number of Model T Fords were exported to China. A year before his death in 1925, Dr. Sun Yat-sen wrote to Henry Ford, inviting him to help build an automotive industry in China. Ford shipped its first automobile to China in 1927, and opened a sales and service branch in Shanghai in 1928, but never set up any manufacturing plants. After that period (possibly because of the turmoil in China and the Great Depression at home), Ford focused its attention on the U.S. market and elsewhere, until the reform period in the late 1970s in China. At that time, Deng Xiaoping personally met with Henry Ford II, prompting Ford to set up an Office of China Affairs at their headquarters. But it was not until 1992 that Ford opened a representative office in Beijing, long after American Motors Corporation (AMC) and Volkswagen had begun producing automobiles on the Chinese mainland. Even then, Ford failed to land a major passenger-car joint-venture agreement with a Chinese partner for another nine years. Because production of the first model at Chang'An Ford did not actually begin until 2003, this chapter mainly assesses the role of technology transfer in the Chang'An-Ford joint-venture negotiations (see figure 7.1).

Ford is headquartered in Dearborn, Michigan. Founded in 1903, it had annual sales of US$171 billion and employed 327,531 people worldwide in 2005 (*Standard & Poor's Register of Corporations* 2005b). Aside from the Ford-brand vehicles, its other automotive brands include Lincoln, Mazda, Mercury, Land Rover, Aston Martin, Jaguar, and Volvo. Its automotive-related services include Ford Credit, Quality Care, Hertz, and Motorcraft.

In the early 1990s, the Chinese government decided to open up its largest domestic producer of passenger cars, Shanghai Automotive Industry Corporation (SAIC), to foreign investment. Both Ford and GM bid on the joint-venture partnership, and ultimately, Ford lost. After its bid was rejected, Ford waited to pursue other partners since it felt the Chinese government was unlikely to approve another major foreign investment soon after the SAIC joint venture. Meanwhile, Honda took over Peugeot's investment in Guangzhou, and Fiat Auto of Italy, Kia

Figure 7.1
New Chang'An Ford factory in Chongqing (photo by author)

Motor of South Korea, and Yulon of Taiwan (25 percent owned by Nissan) all formed new joint ventures with Chinese firms.

After losing the SAIC opportunity, Ford invested in six joint ventures related to manufacturing parts and components in China, but these businesses were spun off in 2000 (Hu 1999). In 1995, the company established Ford Motor China Ltd. That same year, Ford bought a 20 percent stake in Jiangling Motors Corporation, and licensed the relevant technology to China for production of a small bus, known internationally as the Transit, in Jiangling's facilities. Production of the Transit began on December 12, 1997. In 1998, Ford increased its stake in Jiangling to 30 percent.

Ford also indirectly invested in China through Mazda, which is 33.3 percent owned by Ford. Mazda has been outsourcing production of its Mazda Premacy at First Auto Works Hainan Motor Company (FCH) since June 2001 and the Mazda 323, known as the Familia, since July 2002 (Kyodo News Service 2002). Mazda started producing its Mazda 6 midsized sedan in 2003. Chang'An, Ford, and Mazda also set up a new vehicle-assembly plant and engine company in Nanjing in 2005 (AFX Asia 2005).

Meanwhile, like many other foreign firms, Ford was only marginally successful in overcoming the high Chinese import tariffs, exporting a total of only 15,000 cars to China from 1990 to 2002. Mostly, Ford has exported the Mondeo Ghia-X from its plant in Taiwan to China, but it has also exported the Lincoln Towncar, Ford Taurus, and Ford Windstar minivan to China (Asia Pulse 2002; Avery 2002).

While Ford was casting about for an opportunity to enter the Chinese passenger-car market, the U.S. government was engaged in negotiations with the Chinese government regarding Permanent Normal Trade Relations (PNTR) status and the related terms of entry for China's accession to the World Trade Organization (WTO). These negotiations would have great bearing on any joint venture that Ford might negotiate thereafter, because the U.S. Trade Representative (USTR) was pressing China to loosen or eliminate many of the restrictions traditionally placed on foreign investors, particularly in the automotive sector. The bilateral PNTR negotiations were concluded in 1999, long before Ford signed the deal with Chang'An for its first major automotive joint venture. The U.S.

Congress subsequently approved the PNTR agreement, and it entered into force in 2000. As discussed in chapters 3 and 4, the agreement specified many changes in Chinese government policy for the automobile sector, including the elimination of conditions on foreign direct investment, such as requirements on technology transfer, local content, and export performance. Ford actively called for the elimination of restrictions on foreign direct investment in the name of the free market. In a 2002 speech in China, for example, Ford President Nick Scheele asserted, "If foreign auto companies, such as Ford Motor Company, are allowed to hold more than 50 percent interests in joint ventures in China, Chinese autos will become more competitive internationally" (ChinaOnline 2002).

After PNTR was signed into law, in April 2001 Ford finally concluded negotiations for a US$98 million joint-venture agreement with Chang'An Automobile (Group) Corp., based in Chongqing, Sichuan Province. The ownership of the joint venture is split equally between the U.S. and Chinese partners. Chang'An agreed to invest US$23.5 million in the joint venture using cash and other assets, and its parent, Chang'An Automotive Group Liability Co. Ltd., agreed to contribute the remainder of the investment on the Chinese side. Ford agreed to contribute US$49 million worth of cash and assets (Dow Jones International News 2001). Chang'An Ford's annual production capacity was initially limited to 50,000 automobiles, a number that could be increased later if there is sufficient demand.

Chang'An was founded in 1862 as the Shanghai Western-Style Artillery Bureau in the treaty port of Shanghai, but eventually was moved to its current location in Chongqing (see figure 7.2). Using its experience with artillery production, Chang'An gradually began producing other types of machinery. It was renamed the State-Owned Chang'An Machine Building Plant in 1953, and it produced its first automobile in 1958 using technology imported from the Soviet Union. This first vehicle was a World War II–era off-road light truck akin to a Jeep, and one of these army-green colored jeeps is still parked in a rear corner of Chang'An's display room at their headquarters. Chang'An produced 1,390 of these light trucks between 1959 and 1963, at which time the factory was closed down. After the Cultural Revolution, this light-truck technology

Figure 7.2
Chang'An headquarters in Chongqing (photo by author)

was transferred to Beijing Automotive Company, future partner of American Motors Corporation (and now DaimlerChrysler).

Chang'An fluctuates between being the fourth- and fifth-largest automobile company in China, and it is the largest producer of minibuses and minitrucks in China (Xinhua Economic News Service 2002). In 2004, it sold 579,091 vehicles, up 40 percent over 2003 (Xinhua Financial January 5, 2005). Chang'An is a subsidiary of the China Commission of Science, Technology, and Industry for National Defense (COSTIND), which reports directly to the State Council. Chang'An is the parent of several vehicle manufacturers, including Hebei Chang'An Automobile Co. Ltd., Nanjing Chang'An Automobile Co. Ltd., Chang'An Victory Automobile Co. Ltd., and the Ford and Suzuki joint ventures (Dow Jones International News 2001; Chang'An Automobile Group 2002).

In 1983, Chang'An commenced automotive production after the Cultural Revolution, licensing minibus technology from the Japanese

Figure 7.3
Ford China salesman at Beijing 2002 Auto Show (photo by author)

company, Suzuki. Chang'An has since become one of China's largest producers of the minibuses, nicknamed *mianbiao* (breadloaf) by the Chinese
due to their resemblance to the shape of a loaf of bread, and minitrucks,
which are versions of the minibuses that have open truck beds in the
back. Thus, Chang'An is probably most famous for its production of
these minis, and when it produced its millionth vehicle on July 21, 2001,
it was a minibus. All of Chang'An's minibuses and minitrucks are produced at its headquarters, a large facility located in the heart of an urban
district of Chongqing. The headquarters comprise stamping, welding,
and assembly plants, as well as testing facilities, company offices, and
the R&D center. Workers on the assembly line appeared busy and well

trained during the summer of 2002, starting up the production line after a brief rest upon the entrance of visitors to the plant. The workers had been taking a break in orange plastic chairs around square tables with matching teacups and a bouquet of flowers alongside the line. These workers receive about US$3,000 per year, plus additional housing assistance.

In 1993, Chang'An formed a manufacturing joint venture to produce subcompact cars with Suzuki called Chongqing Chang'An Suzuki Automobile Corp. The initial registered capital of Chang'An Suzuki was US$59.98 million, and this was later increased to US$70 million (CATARC 2002b). The two cars produced during the time of this study by Chang'An Suzuki were the Alto hatchback (now SC7081) and small Gazelle sedan (now SC7130). The hatchback cost between 43,800 and 61,920 RMB (US$5,342–$7,551), depending on options. The sedans, widely used as yellow taxis in Chongqing, each cost between 74,800 and 135,582 RMB (US$9,122–$16,534).

Ford was interested in Chang'An both because it was one of the largest car companies in China, and because the other major Chinese companies had already formed joint ventures with other competitor foreign firms. Ford knew that the Chinese government would look upon the joint venture favorably for four reasons. First, the government was on a campaign to attract foreign investment in the West. Second, the government was anxious to convert military companies into civilian entities. Third, Ford could introduce alternative-fuel technologies that would capitalize on China's natural-gas reserves found predominantly in areas around Chongqing. Last, Chang'An's management and general track record with respect to working with foreign companies was favorable (telephone interview with K. Davey, director, Business Strategy, Asia Pacific and Africa, Ford Motor Company, Dearborn, MI, 2003).

Chang'An Ford was initially aiming to break into the small to midsized car market in China. Dale Jones, vice president of Marketing, Sales, and Service at Ford China, announced in June 2002 that Chang'An Ford was targeting the burgeoning upper-middle-class consumer with a low-priced car "tailored for the family owner and small business entrepreneur" (Avery 2002). The goal, according to one proud Chang'An official, is to "directly compete with the Buick Sail," which was produced by

Shanghai GM at the time (interview with a Chang'An employee, Chongqing, 2002). The price of the new Ford Fiesta initially ranged between US$10,725 and US$15,435, depending on the engine and transmission, and it was being marketed to people twenty-five to thirty-five years old (Bradsher 2003). Chang'An Ford also began production of the Mondeo midsized sedans in 2003. Due to the subsequent unpopularity of the dated Fiesta, Ford later introduced a version of the Ford Focus in mid-2005. In 2005, the Chinese government granted approval for a new manufacturing plant to be built in Nanjing, which will be owned by Ford, Mazda, and Chang'An Automobile Group (Xinhua Economic News Service 2005a).

Ford's new joint venture with Chang'An had to coexist with the Chang'An-Suzuki joint venture. Interestingly, General Motors owns a 20 percent stake in Suzuki, so Chang'An is a partner, albeit indirectly, to the two firms most directly competitive in the U.S. market.

Good Enough for China

In the joint-venture company that produced the Fiesta, Ford transferred all of the automotive technology, along with the design of the manufacturing plant, to Chang'An. Together they built a new set of facilities in the new high-tech industrial area near the airport in Chongqing. Workers were trained in Ford's India plant, and production of the Fiesta commenced in early 2003. According to sources from both Chang'An and Ford, the technology-transfer process for the Ford Fiesta was smooth. The relative ease of the technology transfer was attributed to mutual interests in getting the Fiesta into production as quickly as possible (interview with a Chang'An employee, Chongqing, 2002).

Early on, there were conflicting accounts of exactly which model was chosen for China, but all essentially led toward Ford's basic small car designed for the international market: a "Fiesta-based" Ikon model. In the end, *Fiesta* was chosen as the model name. Reports from the Indian media indicate that the model is actually a version of the Ford Ikon, which is based on the Fiesta platform, and is in production at the Ford India plant in Chennai. David Friedman, managing director and president of Ford India, said in June 2002 that the workforce in the Chinese plant "needs to be taught how to make the Ikon," and that Ford India is helping in these training efforts (quoted in Ramakrishnan 2002). Interestingly, when he announced the joint venture in April 2001, Chang'An President Yin Jiaxu denied that the chosen model would be the Ikon (Gong 2001).

Friedman of Ford India said that "almost 99 percent of the car will be the same as that made here [in India]. There will be minor changes to the grille, especially to suit the local taste. The Chinese also prefer a different kind of seat fabric" (quoted in Ramakrishnan 2002). The only major change from the India model is that the car must be adapted for left-hand drive. According to other reports, Ford has made more than 200 changes (some probably very small) to the model to adapt it for Chinese conditions, including adoption of an automatic transmission (Auto Asia 2002). It is, therefore, the first Ford car on a Fiesta platform to use an automatic transmission (Treece 2002b).

The Ford Fiesta was launched in the United States in 1973, in the wake of the first oil shock, as Ford's first front-wheel-drive compact car. Until that time, Ford's leadership had been adamantly opposed to the production of smaller cars (Halberstam 1986). No longer produced in the United States, modified versions of the Fiesta continue to be produced in and for foreign markets. A new Fiesta model was introduced in Europe in 2000, but the versions produced in South Africa, India, and China date from older generations.

Thus, the Ford Fiesta technology in production in China is not necessarily "old," but neither is it particularly "new." Indeed, it appears that Ford is bringing more modern technology to Chang'An than it ever received from Suzuki, but the Fiesta is far from the "cutting edge." Initially, it was estimated that 62 percent of the parts for the model would be made domestically in China (ChinaOnline 2001). Most of the other parts were to be imported into China from India and shipped three days up the Yangtze River from Shanghai to the western province of Sichuan, where the plant is located. In August 2002, Ford India began exporting parts to the Chongqing plant, and it plans to export regulators, steering columns, horns, some chassis components, hinges, brackets, hoses, gearshift knobs, and smaller metal parts to China. Ford India also exports complete knockdown (CKD) kits of the Ikon to South Africa, Mexico, and Brazil (Business Line 2002).

The size of the Fiesta's engine was restricted to certain specifications because in order for Chang'An Ford to technically avoid competition with the Chang'An Suzuki joint venture, it must produce cars with engines *larger* than 1.3 liters. All the Chang'An Suzuki cars have engines *smaller* than 1.3 liters. Thus, the Fiesta was produced with a 1.6-liter engine. An ironic twist to these fine distinctions is that since Suzuki is 20 percent owned by General Motors (producer of the Shanghai GM Buick Sail, which has a 1.6-liter engine), the two joint-venture partners are indirectly competing with each other anyway.

The technological capabilities of Chang'An appear to be limited to manufacturing capabilities, and most of Chang'An's knowledge about the manufacturing process was acquired through its partnership with Suzuki. Before establishing a joint venture with Suzuki, Chang'An initially licensed Suzuki's technology in 1983, beginning production in 1984. However, the technology was dated and of undetermined 1970s vintage. Once a formal joint venture was established in 1993, Suzuki transferred all the relevant automotive technology to Chang'An to produce a small sedan with a 0.8-liter engine called the Alto (the 7080 model). This technology was also of late 1970s to early 1980s vintage, which Chang'An Suzuki modified very slightly with changes to the ignition and front-end body structure over the years. In 1998, Suzuki transferred a newer model to replace the Alto, called the *Lingyiang* (Gazelle). There are two versions of this model, one of which has a 1.0-liter engine (F Series) and one has a 1.3-liter engine (G Series).

Thus, through its joint venture with Suzuki, Chang'An acquired solid production capabilities, but according to one engineer there, it is still "behind" in design and experimentation. He said that they now know more about what they *don't* know, and this gave Chang'An more bargaining power in its negotiations with Ford. When Chang'An first negotiated with Suzuki, it received "very low levels of technological content because we didn't know anything" (interview with a Chang'An employee, Chongqing, 2002). This same engineer believed that Chang'An was getting relatively current "hard" technologies from Ford, but as of 2002, the workers had received much less training than they previously received from Suzuki.

The Chang'An representative expressed hope that Ford would learn from Suzuki because in his opinion, "Suzuki kept its promises." He added that Chang'An would like to collaborate in a joint R&D center for Chongqing with Ford but that so far, this had not been agreed on. Ford China said they agreed to develop plans for longer-term capability within the joint venture, based on specific business needs. In the past, other companies may have been mandated to establish technical centers up front, but Ford knew that WTO rules prohibited the Chinese government from requiring technology transfer (telephone interview with K. Davey, Dearborn, MI, 2003). It seems especially unlikely that Ford will agree to such a center because Ford recently established its first research center in Asia (and fifth in the world), the Design and Research Center at Ford Lio Ho Motor Company in Taiwan, worth NT$10 billion (US$287 million) (China Post 2002).

On the other hand, Ford has a history of investing in Chinese technological capabilities that dates back to the historic meeting between Henry Ford and Deng Xiaoping in the late 1970s. At that time, a Ford Visiting Scientists program was established with the goal of annually bringing five to ten Chinese scientists to Dearborn, Michigan, for up to two years. Since the 1990s, at any given time Ford has been investing in fifteen to thirty basic and applied research projects at Chinese institutes and universities. Ford does not make similar research investments in Chang'An, but it does do training for workers to facilitate the manufacturing process, including management know-how for professional and technical staffs (telephone interview with K. Davey, Dearborn, MI, 2003).

According to a senior Ford official, there are a number of reasons why Ford might invest more seriously in Chinese technological capabilities in the future. First, investment in local technological capability is an important factor in understanding market needs, recruiting talented people, understanding government regulations, and so forth. Second, as long as there is a significant cost advantage to investing in researchers in Chinese academic institutions, it makes sense to develop more capabilities in China. Third, Ford believes that the Chinese market could be as large as the North American market by 2020, and Ford has always believed that one should build where one sells. Every market has unique characteristics, and salaries and wages earned in developing countries and building automotive products creates higher demand for those products (telephone interview with K. Davey, Dearborn, MI, 2003).

Thus, aside from the technology transfer that Chang'An negotiates from its foreign partners, Chang'An will have to continue to rely on its own technical expertise for innovation. This center received 3 percent of annual sales for its budget, totaling 333 million RMB (US$38 million) in 2001 (interview with a Chang'An employee, Chongqing, 2002).

Ford had not yet encountered any intellectual property rights issues in its joint venture with Chang'An as of 2002. From Ford's point of view, this is partly because the Chinese do not yet have sufficient capabilities to reverse engineer an entire car, and also because Ford and Chang'An are establishing a relationship of trust with a shared understanding of the value and competitive advantage of protecting technology. In other sectors such as motorcycles and parts, when the technological content is lower, there is greater leakage of intellectual property (telephone interview with K. Davey, Dearborn, MI, 2003).

Environmentally, all of the automobiles produced in the Chang'An Suzuki joint venture are purportedly capable of meeting EURO II air-pollution standards, which are required in China's largest cities. Chang'An installs catalytic converters that they developed with the Netherlands on all their cars. Similarly, the Ford Fiesta being produced by Chang'An Ford was required to meet EURO II standards. Also, since the Fiesta is a small and lightweight car, it is reasonably fuel efficient. One Ford official commented that the Chinese Fiesta's fuel efficiency was 10–15 percent worse than the European Fiesta, mainly reflecting differences in fuel quality between China and Europe (telephone interview with K. Davey, Dearborn, MI, 2003). Yet, according to company public relations materials, the Ford Fiesta is advertised as getting 26 miles per gallon in Europe for urban driving, and 32 miles per gallon in China for urban driving—but these comparisons are hard to make without independent testing using the same driving cycle.

Chang'An's domestic R&D group is working on hybrid-electric vehicle development as part of a high-tech research program established by the

Ministry of Science and Technology (MOST) to develop cleaner automotive technology for China without any assistance from Ford or Suzuki. Initially, Chang'An was not included in the government program, but after expressing sincere interest, they were admitted. A Chang'An engineer said that Chang'An funds 70 percent of their clean-vehicle research and 30 percent is funded by MOST. They also closely collaborate with Tsinghua and Liaoning Universities on technology development. Chang'An plans to use the Suzuki Gazelle as a platform for its hybrid vehicle. Suzuki has agreed to help with technology development, but had not done so as of 2002. Chang'An was also working on the development of natural-gas-based vehicles in order to take advantage of the rich reserves of natural gas in the region at the time.

Revamping the Strategy

The Ford Fiesta in production at the new Chang'An Ford plant in Chongqing, Sichuan, is neither new nor old. It is more modern than the technology previously in production at Chang'An's domestic minibus and Suzuki plants, and it could be characterized as "midlife" technology. Yet Ford's China car is far from the cutting edge, and quite far behind U.S. levels in terms of pollution-control equipment. It does not contain any advanced fuel-economy technologies, although because of its size, it is a reasonably fuel-efficient car in comparison with larger conventional sedans.

Ford's primary aim is to establish a local manufacturing base in China to produce compact cars for the domestic market alone. It might become an export base in the future because of good labor costs and the supply base that is already in place. Ford's other plants in Taiwan and India are more likely to export to other markets than its China plant is. Ford does not view its partner as a source of innovation, but rather as a partner in manufacturing. In this case study, a number of barriers to the transfer of cleaner advanced technology to China can be observed. Both Chang'An and the Chinese government (at either the municipal or central level) failed to ask for significantly more advanced technologies, and Ford felt no obligation to transfer them. In addition, Ford initially had real concerns about leakage of intellectual property, although in reality,

Ford has encountered few intellectual property problems. As of 2005, it was too soon to know if Ford will update and refresh the technology it transfers to China.

Unless Chang'An asks for more advanced technologies and acquires enough bargaining power to persuade Ford to make the transfer of these technologies, there seems to be little motivation for Ford to do so, other than to strengthen its position in the Chinese market. Incentives for more advanced technology transfer, from Ford's point of view, have more to do with competition and the preferences of the Chinese consumer than with the requests for more advanced technology from its Chinese partner. Ford is entering a fairly competitive market in the compact class with a number of small cars already on the streets, namely, the Toyota Vios, the Buick Sail, the domestic Geely sedan, and the VW Polo. This competition for discerning consumers seems to be the most likely incentive for technological improvement in Chang'An Ford's products. As a Ford representative commented, "Fuel economy is driven by competition in China." Another incentive for technology transfer is the increasing availability of higher-quality and low-cost parts and components in China. If automotive parts can readily be sourced locally, then the costs of technology transfer can be reduced, which eliminates one barrier for technology transfer.

8

Technology Transfer, Energy, and the Environment

If the Chinese wish to deploy substantially cleaner and more efficient automobiles in China, they face a fundamental choice about the extent to which they "make" or the extent to which they "buy" the cleaner technologies. Historically, the Chinese were forced to buy conventional automotive technologies from abroad because their own technological capabilities were limited. The idea was that they would learn through technology transfer and gradually acquire their own technological capabilities, eventually attaining some self-sufficiency (Harwit 1995). China finds itself in a similar predicament today because it lacks the advanced technological capabilities needed for clean-vehicle development and deployment. Based on its past experience, is it wise for China to rely on a strategy of technology transfer to acquire cleaner automotive technologies from abroad? If so, which cleaner technologies should China purchase from abroad, and which should China try to make domestically? To answer these questions, lessons can be derived from analyzing the three U.S.-China automobile joint ventures from 1984 to 2002: Beijing Jeep, Shanghai GM, and Chang'An Ford.

Based on the empirical evidence from these cases, three main findings emerge from this research:

• U.S. firms transferred outdated automotive pollution-control technologies during the 1980s and 1990s to China because no Chinese policies were in place to require cleaner or more energy-efficient technologies.

• To some extent, U.S. foreign direct investment helped to deploy cleaner automotive technologies in China than those that were in use before, but the potential environmental benefit of the newer technologies is being offset by the growth in the total number of cars on the road.

• Automotive technologies that were transferred were not necessarily updated in tandem with updates made to equivalent foreign models, again due to lack of incentives (policy or otherwise) to do so.

One further important implication can be drawn from this study: leapfrogging to substantially cleaner automotive technologies through technology transfer from foreign firms is likely to be quite challenging for the Chinese automobile industry without serious efforts to align incentives to provoke cleaner and more efficient automotive production and consumption.

Environmental Performance and Fuel Efficiency

This section will compare the environmental performance and fuel efficiency in Beijing Jeep, Shanghai GM, and Chang'An Ford. An automobile can be made "cleaner" through a combination of three measures: reducing tailpipe emissions of air pollutants, improving fuel efficiency, and using cleaner fuels. Tailpipe emissions of common air pollutants including nitrogen oxides (NO_x), carbon monoxide (CO), and hydrocarbons (HC) are usually controlled through catalyst technology and onboard diagnostic (OBD) systems. Cleaner fuels—such as unleaded, low-sulfur, or compressed natural gas—can also contribute to reducing some of the harmful emissions of pollutants from an automobile. Emissions of the main greenhouse gas, carbon dioxide (CO_2), can be reduced through better fuel efficiency and, to some extent, from switching from petroleum-based fuels to compressed natural gas (which contains less carbon in relation to its energy content). Net carbon emissions can also be reduced by using alcohol fuels derived from biomass (which removes carbon dioxide from the atmosphere when the crops are growing).

Electric vehicles and vehicles powered by fuel cells operated on hydrogen are sometimes described as being clean, but their overall cleanliness depends on how the electricity or hydrogen is obtained. Worldwide, hydrogen is usually produced from natural gas (with associated release of greenhouse gases to the atmosphere). In China, hydrogen would probably be produced from coal since coal is China's most abundant energy resource. Most electricity in China is generated by burning coal. Of course, whatever the origin of the primary energy for vehicle propulsion, increasing the energy efficiency of the automobile can not only reduce greenhouse-gas emissions, but also reduce emissions of conventional pollutants as well.

The finding that U.S. manufacturers transferred outdated automotive pollution-control technologies mainly applies to the tailpipe-emission-control technologies in the 1980s and 1990s, because the situation with respect to fuel economy (and therefore carbon emissions) is unclear due to the lack of independent, standardized data.

Environmental Performance

By U.S. or European standards, each of the U.S. auto manufacturers examined in the case studies transferred outdated automotive tailpipe pollution-control technologies to China and continues to do so, but it is important to note that the manufacturers have always been in compliance with Chinese law (see table 2.2). Although the automobiles produced by the joint ventures all abide by Chinese law, they would fail to meet current air-pollution-control standards in the United States, Japan, or Europe. In other words, none of the U.S. firms transferred pollution-control technology that is equivalent to the equipment installed in cars sold to consumers in richer countries. The pollution-control technology transferred to China by the U.S. manufacturers is about one decade behind that used in Europe, Japan, and the United States.

As discussed in chapter 2, Chinese regulations for tailpipe-emission control were first set in 2000, the same year that the Chinese government banned leaded fuel and required catalytic converters to be installed in all new automobiles. China adopted the European Union's system of regulating automotive air pollution, such that as of 2000, all automotive manufacturers in China were required to meet EURO I standards (required in Europe as of 1992; see table 2.2). In 2004, auto manufacturers were required to meet EURO II standards, which was the level required in Europe as of 1994. In Beijing and some other major cities, manufacturers were required to meet EURO III standards as of July 2005, and in 2007, China will require all new autos to meet EURO III standards, the level required by Europe in 2000. In interviews and in their public relations materials, Shanghai GM and Chang'An Ford representatives declared that all their vehicles met EURO II standards as of

2002 (see table 8.1). Beijing Jeep officials said that their vehicles were EURO II compliant, except for the Jeep Grand Cherokee, which they reported met EURO III standards. China, like most other developing countries, does not regulate carbon dioxide emissions, but it started doing so indirectly in 2005 with its imposition of its first fuel-economy standards.

Fuel Efficiency

China imposed its first fuel-economy standards in July 2005, as discussed in chapter 2. Through 2002, manufacturers in China were not required to report the fuel efficiency of the vehicles they produce, which made it nearly impossible to gather reliable and standard data. In interviews or through public relations material, fuel-efficiency data were obtained

Table 8.1
Environmental performance comparisons 1985–2002

	Beijing Jeep	Shanghai GM	Chang'An Ford
Emission-Control Standard Met[a]	EURO II, Grand Cherokee EURO III	All models EURO II with 80,000-mile guarantee	EURO II
Grants	None	Some R&D funding to universities and institutes related to environmental performance of automobiles.	Some R&D funding to Chinese universities. Also Ford sponsors an "Environment Protection Prize" program in China.
Other	None	PATAC has national emission testing center; GM paid for SEPA study on phaseout of leaded fuel, sponsored workshop on OBD technology, and donated EV car to China.	Chang'An approached Ford about collaborating on CNG-based technologies, but Ford has not agreed to do this yet. Ford sponsored two workshops on automotive emission control.

[a] As reported by manufacturer in interviews. All data from interviews with company officials in Detroit (May 2002), Beijing and Chongqing (June 2002), and Shanghai (July 2002), as well as from follow-up communications.

directly from the manufacturers, but these data could not be independently verified or standardized. An attempt has been made to standardize the data so that all numbers are based on an urban driving cycle, but the results can only be considered preliminary until better data are available (see table 8.2).

Taking these data limitations into account, it appears that the fuel efficiency of each automobile produced in China prior to 2002 was roughly similar to its foreign-model equivalent, with the possible exception of the Ford Fiesta. Without independent and standardized testing, it is not possible to analyze this further. There is one instance where the fuel efficiency of a Chinese model was purportedly improved after being released to the Chinese market, when Shanghai GM introduced a more fuel-efficient Buick New Century to meet consumer demands. Shanghai GM claims that its Chinese model is actually slightly more fuel efficient than the U.S. equivalent, but this assertion could not be verified.

The story with respect to greenhouse-gas carbon dioxide is the same. The greenhouse-gas emissions of U.S. and Chinese equivalent models appear to be quite similar, with the possible exception of the Ford Fiesta.

Why U.S. Firms Did Not Transfer Cleaner Technologies

A primary finding from this research is that all of the U.S. firms transferred outdated automotive pollution-control technologies to their partners in China when the Chinese had no pollution-control laws for passenger cars (prior to 2000). Five explanations for why cleaner technologies were not transferred can be identified. First and most important, there simply were no compelling incentives for the U.S. firms to do so. The Chinese government issued no foreign-investment policies that directly required cleaner technologies to be transferred. Nor did the Chinese government pass environmental laws that required significantly cleaner technologies to be introduced into China to meet Chinese domestic standards. Second, the Chinese companies did not bargain for these technologies in their joint-venture negotiations either. Third, China's relatively weak environmental movement may be partly to blame. Fourth, the lack of incentives in contract, law, or policy can either be attributed to a vicious circle related to domestic competitiveness or to a marriage

Table 8.2

Fuel-economy comparisons between Chinese and U.S. models as of 2002

Model	Fuel efficiency in Chinese model in urban driving (mpg)	Fuel efficiency in U.S. or European equivalent model for urban driving (mpg)[a]
Buick New Century[b]	18–21	20
Buick Sail[b]	23–26	27.2
Jeep Grand Cherokee[c]	14	14
Jeep Cherokee[c]	18–21	16
Jeep BJ2020[c]	17	No equivalent
Ford Fiesta[d]	32	26

[a] The U.S. figures are as rated by EPA in 2002 (except for the Ford Fiesta and Opel Corsa) in miles per gallon (mpg). When Chinese data were reported using constant high speeds (such as 60 km/hour), they were adjusted to be 40 percent less efficient for "city" driving.

[b] The U.S. equivalent to the Chinese New Century is the Buick Century 2002. The Chinese New Century has a 2.5-liter engine and the U.S. model has a 3.1-liter engine, both with six cylinders. The Buick Sail's EU equivalent is the five-door UK Opel Corsa Elegance, which has a 1.4 L engine compared with the Sail's V4 1.6 L engine.

[c] The Jeep Grand Cherokee in China and the United States are both automatic V8 4.7 L engines, but the Chinese version is all-wheel drive (AWD) and the U.S. version is 4WD. The China Jeep Cherokee (2.5 L manual) is no longer produced in the United States, so a 2002 Jeep Liberty 4WD manual V6 3.7 L model was used for comparison. The BJ2020 model is a manual transmission with a V8 2.4 L engine.

[d] The Ford Fiesta is not sold in the United States, so a United kingdom model was used for comparison. Both have auto 1.6 L engines. In an interview, one Ford official said that the fuel efficiency of the Chinese Fiesta is 10 percent–15 percent worse than its European equivalent due to fuel-efficiency differences.

Data sources: www.beijing-jeep.com; www.ford.com/cn/fiesta.newcar/1-1-a.html; *interview with P. Murtaugh at Shanghai GM (July 2002)*; http://buypower.vauxhall.co.uk (*technical specifications for Corsa Elegance as given above*); www.ford.co.uk/ie/fiesta/fie-specs_drvtc/fie_specs_fuel.

of convenience between the Chinese government and foreign auto companies. Fifth, the U.S. auto companies knew that the quality of the Chinese fuels was so poor that if they were to transfer more advanced air-pollution-control technologies, these technologies would be rendered ineffectual by the low-quality fuel. Each of these five explanations will be now explored in more detail, along with the evidence.

Lack of Policy or Legal Incentives

The first reason that U.S. firms did not transfer cleaner technologies to China is that there were insufficient policy and legal incentives. As of 2002, Wei-Ming Soh of DaimlerChrysler China was so sure that the Chinese government would not impose stringent environmental standards (to the extent that they would be difficult for DaimlerChrysler to meet) that he "doesn't even think about it at this point in time" (interview with W.-M. Soh, vice president, Special Projects, BJC Sales and Marketing, DaimlerChrysler, Beijing, 2002). This outlook was reflected among all three U.S. manufacturers because none of them were at all worried that Chinese environmental policy would become a technological challenge or barrier for their joint-venture operations. If Chinese environmental policy did mandate stricter controls on automotive emissions or fuel economy, there is little question that the U.S. firms would immediately comply. As Kristen Zimmerman of GM noted, "If there is an environmental policy already in place then GM, by all means, will comply. But GM would choose first to work with the Chinese government to develop an environmental policy based on the progress and learning mechanisms inherent in voluntary initiatives rather than develop an environmental policy based on reactive measures in response to mandatory, binding targets" (interview with K. Zimmerman, Detroit, 2002).

The complete lack of concern on the part of the U.S. manufacturers about being able to comply with Chinese environmental laws demonstrates that environmental factors not only rank low on the list of U.S. investor concerns about China, but also that foreign firms do not anticipate that Chinese environmental policy will be a future constraining factor for them. In other words, the U.S. firms simply feel no pressure to transfer more advanced environmental technologies. Chinese standards for automotive emission control do not provide sufficient incentive for U.S. firms to transfer significantly cleaner or more fuel-efficient automotive technologies.

The literature contains at least four theoretical explanations that might bear on why U.S. multinational firms might transfer outdated automotive pollution-control technologies to a developing country like China: the "pollution-haven," "race-to-the-bottom," "stuck-in-the-mud," and "pollution-halo" hypotheses. The pollution-haven hypothesis posits that multinational corporations will relocate to developing countries because of lower environmental-compliance costs. The race-to-the-bottom hypothesis is that developing countries will weaken their environmental standards to attract foreign direct investment (FDI), placing pressure on the industrialized countries to weaken their standards as well, in order to compete with the developing countries. A variation on this theory is the stuck-in-the-mud hypothesis (Zarsky 1999b), which argues that developing countries will not raise environmental standards for fear of losing FDI to other countries. In contrast, the pollution-halo hypothesis asserts that FDI will bring cleaner environmental technology and improved environmental-management practices to developing countries.

Despite the finding that U.S. firms are not transferring their best-available environmental technologies, the Sino-U.S. joint ventures do not appear to be examples of the pollution havens or a race to the bottom. This study finds no evidence that China's weaker air-pollution standards affected any of the U.S. firms' decisions to invest there. Instead, U.S. companies primarily invested in China because they wanted to gain access to the Chinese market (which was virtually closed to imports when they invested), not because Chinese environmental standards were lax. This finding is in accordance with other studies that have found no evidence for a pollution haven in developing countries (Chudnovsky and Lopez 2002; Gallagher 2004). As Zarsky (1999a, p. 19) notes, "Differences in environmental standards and/or abatement costs have apparently not made a significant difference to firm location decisions." There is also no evidence for the race-to-the-bottom hypothesis because the Chinese did not lower their standards to attract FDI (environmental standards were nonexistent to begin with). To the contrary, the Chinese government has announced a progressive tightening of national emission standards for air-pollution control to the EURO IV level, and appears intent on harmonizing its standards with those of advanced industrialized countries.

For the same reason, there is also no evidence for the stuck-in-the-mud hypothesis. Chinese government officials do not appear to be particularly concerned about how the regulations might affect the international competitiveness of their firms. This lack of concern could be because China is not exporting any significant number of automobiles. The government is more concerned about competitiveness in the domestic market (see the "vicious-circle" discussion below). Yet, it is possible to imagine that environmental policies could get "trapped in the mainstream," such that Chinese officials might hesitate to promulgate regulations that go beyond the levels in industrialized countries, especially if such actions were perceived by China's competitors to be nontariff barriers to trade under WTO rules. In fact, if the Chinese government were pushing the technological frontier with its environmental policies, it would likely encounter substantial resistance from foreign and domestic firms alike.

Finally, there is no compelling evidence of a "pollution halo" in the Chinese automobile industry either. U.S. firms did bring cleaner environmental technology to China than was in production there before, but the technology was only marginally better, and it was not transferred until Chinese law required better environmental performance.

Weak Bargaining by Chinese Firms

It will be interesting to analyze the effect of China's new fuel-economy regulations. The first phase that started in 2005 is not considered challenging by any standard, but the Phase II of the regulations in 2008 will exert some real pressure to improve fuel efficiency, especially on larger, heavier vehicles (assuming the standards are vigorously enforced). Although the new fuel-economy standards are more aggressive than those in the United States, they are nowhere close to the European or Japanese standards, and so are unlikely to provoke the transfer of substantially more fuel-efficient technologies (i.e., hybrid-electric vehicles) alone. More stringent standards would be needed to motivate the transfer of such technologies. Alternatively, the Chinese government could use fiscal incentives such as tax breaks for owners of highly fuel-efficient vehicles or fuel taxes to encourage a shift toward more efficient vehicles.

The second reason that U.S. firms did not transfer cleaner technologies to China is that the Chinese government-owned automobile firms undermined themselves in joint-venture talks with the foreign companies when negotiating for advanced technologies, especially cleaner technologies. This is perhaps the biggest enduring puzzle. Why did China not demand more advanced technologies, and especially cleaner technologies, given its current concerns about urban air pollution and oil imports? Due to concerns about intellectual property rights and creating future competitors, it is unsurprising (although perhaps disappointing) that U.S. firms did not magnanimously offer cleaner technologies to their Chinese partners. Why should they volunteer state-of-the-art technology to these partners? Yet there was significant variation among the U.S. firms in terms of the modernity of the technologies transferred, and this variation deserves exploration.

Six main explanations emerge from this research for why the Chinese auto firms did not bargain harder during their joint-venture negotiations, as listed in table 8.3. First, there was inconsistent central-government policy guidance during the times each joint venture was negotiated, and this mainly explains the variation among the three cases. Second, there is evidence that at times the Chinese firms did not really know what to ask for from their foreign partner. Third, the Chinese knew that their own technological capabilities were weak, and so in some cases they felt they had no right to ask for more advanced technologies. Fourth, they often felt so powerless in the joint-venture negotiations that they did not dare ask for more. Fifth, in one case, the Chinese correctly believed it

Table 8.3
Explanations for weak bargaining by Chinese firms for more advanced technology from their U.S. partners

Explanation	Beijing Jeep	Shanghai GM	Chang'An Ford
Weak government guidance	✓		✓
Naïveté about options	✓	✓	✓
Questions of propriety	✓	✓	✓
Feeling powerless	✓		✓
Questions of legality			✓
Local government interests		✓	✓

was illegal to demand technology transfer because of WTO rules. Sixth, it has also been argued that Chinese firms owned by local governments tend to undermine the larger interests of the national industry during joint-venture negotiations by only considering their narrower commercial interests rather than the industrial interests of the nation as a whole (Harwit 1995; Bowditch 1998). There is some evidence for this argument about the influence of local governments.

In the early case of Beijing Jeep, the Chinese felt that they had virtually no capabilities, and indeed they did not; Beijing Automotive Industry Company (BAIC) was totally reliant on the foreign firm for new technology. At the time, the Chinese government had not issued any specific policies for the auto sector and related investment, so BAIC had no government guidance with respect to automotive technology other than the internal directive to obtain a completely new design for a soft-top, military, all-terrain vehicle. Although BAIC asked for the military design, BAIC eventually settled for AMC's Jeep Cherokee. BAIC did not know which particular technologies to specify for transfer, so it just accepted that the Cherokee would be sent to China on a complete knockdown kit (CKD) basis. Even when DaimlerChrysler renegotiated its contract with BAIC twenty years later, Daimler received "no specific request from both the Chinese partner and the government as per which technologies should be transferred." Instead, according to Wei-Ming Soh, the choice of technology depended more on market demand and the ability of Beijing Jeep to maintain specific quality levels in their products (interview with W.-M. Soh, Beijing, 2002).

During its joint-venture negotiations in the mid-1990s, Shanghai Automotive Industry Corporation (SAIC) bargained harder than any other Chinese firm to date, with mixed success, for a number of reasons. First, SAIC had not gleaned much technological knowledge from its original foreign partner, Volkswagen, during the previous decade. Consequently, SAIC intended to structure its new joint venture with GM to elicit substantive technology transfer and a real investment in the operations. GM was equally interested in focusing on the success of the joint venture itself. SAIC had real legitimacy when bargaining because it was reputed to be the most profitable Chinese automobile firm, and there were numerous foreign suitors anxious to enter into a joint venture with it, including both Ford and Toyota. In addition, SAIC had clear government backing about the imperative for technology transfer. The Chinese government had recently passed the 1994 Auto Industry Law, which placed new and specific requirements on foreign firms regarding technology transfer. So, SAIC's biggest problem was not so much that it did not bargain very hard, but more that it did not know exactly what to ask for from GM, and it certainly was not focused in any case on clean technologies.

In the middle of this continuum lies Chang'An Ford. The parent of Chang'An was so anxious to secure a respectable foreign partner and status as one of the top automotive manufacturers in China that Chang'An felt weak in the negotiations. For Chang'An, it was so important to win Ford's investment that it was afraid to risk squandering the opportunity by being demanding about technology during the negotiations. Moreover, Chang'An understood correctly that it was illegal to make explicit demands about technology transfer because of WTO rules. Indeed, the Chinese government had conceded that it would not place restrictions on technology transfer during its negotiations with the United States prior to China's entry into the WTO. Ford did not feel that it had to bow to any governmental demands to establish a technical center, although the government had stated this desire. Ford did not bring cutting-edge technology to China, but it did not anticipate that other companies would start to do so either. Competition appears to have been the primary motivator with respect to Ford's decision to transfer technology, not hard bargaining on the part of its Chinese partner. Chang'An also did not seem to know what exactly to ask for from Ford since at least one Chang'An official believes that Chang'An received relatively current technology, especially in comparison with its old joint-venture partner, Suzuki. Interestingly, Chang'An Ford's first product, the Ford Fiesta, was criticized in the Chinese media for containing outdated technology, but it is at least newer than the old Suzuki technology. As a Chang'An authority commented, "Suzuki gave [Chang'An] very low technological content because they [Chang'An] didn't know anything" (interview with a Chang'An employee, Chongqing, 2002).

One last hypothesis proffered by a foreign observer working in China for why the Chinese companies do not bargain harder with their U.S.

counterparts is what he called the "good enough phenomenon" (interview with E. Clark, director, Product Engineering, Beijing Jeep Corporation, Beijing, 2002). For many years, and perhaps still today, the Chinese were content just to get access to the product—the car itself. Acquisition of the related technological knowledge was a secondary goal, if even a goal at all. So long as the car was cheap, functional, and sold reasonably well, the Chinese companies were satisfied. Jia Xinguang, analyst with the China National Automotive Industry Consulting and Development Corporation, captures the sentiment well when he states, "In the current Chinese car market, the most important thing for a foreign carmaker is not that its models are old or new, but that they are suitable for local customers. . . . Volkswagen's Santana and Jetta are the two oldest foreign car models being produced in China, but they are still selling well" (Gong 2003).

Until the late 1990s, there was limited competition from glitzy foreign products so Chinese consumers were forced to simply buy what was available to them, even if it was the same, boring, fifteen-year-old design. Automobiles like the old Soviet-era Beijing Jeep 2020 were deemed "good enough" for the Chinese market, not just by the U.S. firms but also by the Chinese companies themselves. Ford's decision to send in a Fiesta (and Chang'An's acceptance of this model) may be one example of the view that it was "good enough" for China's consumers. GM's decision to rush the Opel Corsa into China to maximize short-term profits instead of designing or adapting a really modern, advanced new car (and SAIC's apparent acceptance of this decision) may be another example of this phenomenon.

Aside from the explanations identified through this research, a number of negotiation theories can help explain why the Chinese firms failed to bargain harder. Contrary to conventional wisdom, a less powerful party is not always at the mercy of the more powerful party because power is specific to any given negotiation (Salacuse 1999). The Chinese firms, however, mostly perceived themselves to be powerless in their individual joint-venture negotiations. Yet negotiating power is the power to convince others through the power of skill, knowledge, commitment, a good relationship, as well as having a good alternative, an elegant solution, and legitimacy (Fisher 1995). The Chinese firms did not seem to recognize these other types of power. Chang'An felt that Ford was the best foreign partner it was likely to attract, and so Chang'An felt a certain desperation to accept Ford's proposals. Similarly, Tianjin FAW Xiali Corporation Ltd felt that it needed Toyota much more than Toyota needed (Tianjin FAW Xiali) because (Tianjin FAW Xiali) was feeling intense competition from SAIC, which had good foreign partners and better technology. So, in the words of one (Tianjin FAW Xiali) employee, "We gave in to everything that Toyota asked" (interview with Chinese engineers at Tianjin Auto Research Institute, Tianjin, 2002). But the Chinese firms may have had more power than they thought. The U.S. firms were very anxious to gain access to the much-vaunted Chinese market of 1.3 billion people. For example, John Smith, GM's president, noted in 1997, "We're positioning ourselves to become a major player in all the growth markets of the world—and especially in the Asia-Pacific region. . . . If China's income growth continues along the path it has been on for the past fifteen years, consider the potential market for cars we could serve" (p. 2). AMC was attracted by China's potentially huge market, and it felt that firms that established a presence in China would be rewarded in the long term (Mann 1989). SAIC clearly realized that it had some power through alternatives because it made GM, Ford, and Toyota bid for the joint venture competitively. Even though Chang'An was afraid that it might not be sufficiently attractive to Ford, it is possible that Ford was just as anxious to woo Chang'An: all the other major foreign manufacturers had already invested in an automotive joint venture in China, and Ford was perceived as late-to-market.

A Relatively Weak Environmental Movement

The third reason that U.S. firms did not transfer cleaner and more efficient technologies to China is that no strong advocacy community was pushing for such technologies in China. Since this study shows, rather bleakly, that very few cleaner automobiles have actually been deployed in China through international technology transfer or otherwise, one must step back and ask whether the Chinese really wanted the deployment of cleaner automobiles in China. Maybe they did not bargain harder for cleaner technologies because they did not really care about them. After all, China faces pressing demands to alleviate poverty, develop the economy, industrialize, and compete with other countries.

Chinese attitudes toward environmental protection are as varied and diverse as they are in any other country. As noted by Yi-Fu Tuan (1973, p. 412), "Among the complex purposes and demands of the real world, attitudes to the environment are no more likely to be consistent than attitudes to people whose company we enjoy on one occasion and find irritating on the next." Ultimately, since the Chinese government controls environmental-advocacy organizations, the power and interests of the automobile industry (which is mostly owned by local governments) currently overwhelm any environmental sentiment that might exist in China.

It has been noted that "most environmental problems have roots in human relationships and are ultimately social, political, and cultural problems" (Shapiro 2001, p. 1). Thus, there is something to be gained by considering Chinese cultural traditions and how they might affect attitudes toward environmental protection in China today. Historically, there have been differing and sometimes contradictory philosophies about the human relationship with the natural environment in China. Taoism, Buddhism, Confucianism, and Communism are four of the most prominent influences in Chinese culture. As one of the oldest continuous civilizations, Chinese society has a long-standing relationship with the land. Traditional rural practices of tilling, water conservation, sustainable harvesting of forests, and nomadic use of grasslands allowed Chinese farmers to farm the land for many centuries (Shapiro 2001). On the other hand, because of its large population, China has always been resource-intensive. For example, as Fairbank (1951, p. 28) notes, "Chinese society and all its mores and institutions have been based from the beginning upon intensive agriculture, which will take the fullest advantage of human labor." As land was exploited and degraded in the north, the Chinese population migrated southward in a steady, but protracted, expansion. As a result, all arable land in China has been completely transformed from its natural state for centuries. Natural disasters, such as torrential floods and excruciating droughts, have repeatedly befallen China, making the control of nature a long-standing preoccupation of Chinese leaders.

In ancient China, primitive animism was chiefly concerned with not disrupting or offending the forces of nature. The notion of *feng shui* (wind and water) derives from this ancient tradition, and it was concerned with the proper placement of human artifacts in relation to nature so as to prevent any harmful disruption. Drawing from this animism, Taoism is the most prominent Chinese tradition clearly reverential toward nature. The mystical Taoists were skeptical of human reason and logic, in contrast to Europeans, who believed that a perfectly rational God had formulated a code of nature's laws that could be deciphered. Taoists believed that until humans learned enough about nature, society could not be properly organized because nature and humans had to coexist in one system (Needham 1969). Buddhism was a foreign religion that came to China between the fourth and eighth centuries A.D. Chinese Buddhists made some adaptations to the religion, but preserved its reverence for all living things. Today, for example, the easiest way to explain that you are a vegetarian in China is simply to say that you are a Buddhist.

The Confucian philosophy is intensely hierarchical, anthropocentric, conservative, and resistant to the unorthodox. Confucians desired to properly order human relations rather than try to understand nature. Confucianism began as a means of bringing social order out of the chaos of the Warring States period, and the philosophy provided a rationale for a strong government bureaucracy (Fairbank 1951). China's strong Confucian tradition of government bureaucracy now both hinders and helps environmental protection there. The State Environmental Protection Administration, for example, is the strongest Chinese advocate for environmental protection, but it is considered to be among the weakest government agencies. In contrast, the National Development and Reform Commission is one of the most powerful government agencies, and it has the core mission of fostering economic growth and development.[1] Confucianism also suppressed dissent and encouraged order, two themes that were picked up and employed later by Chairman Mao and his Communist regime. Still, there are elements of Confucianism that support sustainable development, such as the Confucian adage that "the Master fished with a line but not with a net; when fowling he did not aim at a roosting bird" (Waley 1989, 128).

The ancient Mandate of Heaven seems to derive from both Taoist and Confucian ideologies (although it technically predates Confucius), because the imperial ruler's mandate to rule derived from his ability to maintain a good relationship with nature. To not offend the heavens, the superior ruler maintained order and carefully observed the proper rituals, such as making an annual visit to the Temple of Heaven to offer sacrifices in exchange for a bountiful harvest. If a natural disaster befell China, the ruler was seen as lacking virtue, losing his mandate to rule, and subject to a popular revolution.

The Communists took a strictly utilitarian approach to nature; they were primarily concerned with the exploitation of natural resources to meet social goals. Early Communism in China was dominated by Chairman Mao Zedong, who articulated an extremely adversarial approach to nature in his slogan "Man Must Conquer Nature" (Ren Ding Sheng Tian) (Shapiro 2001, 9). Many of Mao's policies caused significant environmental stress or harm. For example, Mao dictated that with many people, strength is great, so the Chinese people were ordered to bear children to cause China's population to swell and thus deter foreign attacks. During the Great Leap Forward (1958–1960), Mao wanted to catch up to the British in steel production, so he ordered trees to be cut down to fuel backyard furnaces. In 1958 alone, 20 million Chinese peasants were also ordered to dig 110,000 small coal-mine pits to fuel these furnaces. The Great Leap Forward caused a massive famine, so Mao ordered the forests to be cleared and planted with grain, again causing massive deforestation. Later, during the Cultural Revolution beginning in 1966, grain was the only crop farmers were permitted to plant; other crops had to be destroyed (Shapiro 2001).

In the post-Mao reform period, the move to a "market economy with socialist characteristics" has resulted in a new wave of consumerism in China. Similar to the situation in the United States, the desire among Chinese citizens to own an automobile is widespread. In fact, the bigger, shinier, and more powerful the car, the better. In a recent *Newsweek* article, Beijing resident Wang Qishun commented, "We're entering the automobile age—cars are bringing a new culture to China, and I want to explore it" (Liu 2002, 26).

At the same time, there is increasing public and government concern in China about urban air pollution, the crowdedness of city streets, and China's increasingly high reliance on imported oil. In an effort to contain environmental deterioration, the Chinese government has passed more than 100 environmental laws and regulations since 1980 and has created eight major pollution-control programs (Ma and Ortolano 2000), though enforcement of these laws and regulations is sporadic and weak. In a 2002 survey of Beijing residents, 93 percent of the respondents expressed worry about environmental changes, such as the recent mild winters, high temperatures in summer, and sandstorms (Xinhua 2002a). In that same year, Chinese children identified environmental protection as one of their "28 main anxieties" in a national survey (Xinhua 2002c).

Also, one observes a detachment in China between the individual ownership of cars and the environmental problems they cause, similar to the lack of connection one can observe among car owners in the United States. Most consumers in both countries do not believe that their car makes any particular difference to air quality or oil imports—after all, what is one more car? One big difference between China and the United States, however, is that there is no tradition of powerful environmental-advocacy groups in China. Instead, there are currently a number of nongovernmental organizations (NGOs) and "government-organized" nongovernmental organizations (GONGOs) devoted to environmental protection in China. Although the organizations have been characterized as diverse in terms of their political independence and strength (Wu 2002), most focus their efforts on relatively uncontroversial environmental education and consciousness-raising. Environmental-advocacy groups in China rarely directly challenge or criticize the policies of the Chinese government, but they are increasingly exposing inadequate local implementation of national environmental-protection laws. As Elizabeth Economy (2004, 174) notes, "If the government is committed to an active and engaged public effort to protect the environment, especially as a means of overcoming the state's decreasing capacity to meet the country's environmental protection needs, it will need to relax these restrictions and free NGOs to flourish."

More than anything, one observes an incredible drive toward industrialization and modernization in China today, and this goal dominates all others. As one researcher says, "The high-growth, resource-intensive development strategy China has pursued . . . [has] no doubt played a critical role in the deteriorating quality of the environment" (Jahiel 1998, 756). Of course, China's historical traditions also influence attitudes today. In particular, the Maoist legacy is still observable in China:

Mao-era efforts to control humans in nature, and nature in humans, have set the scene for the current precarious environmental situation, which has deteriorated with China's post-Mao push to development. Explosive economic growth and the rush to industrialize are obvious sources of China's unfolding environmental crisis. However, the core dynamics . . . are still at work, albeit in attenuated or altered form. Political repression still marginalizes intellectuals. . . . Urgency still leads to rapid and unsustainable exploitation of natural resources, although now the urgency is to get rich rather than to achieve socialist utopia or continuous revolution. A centralized bureaucracy anxious about its ability to maintain control still promulgates decrees that are formalistically applied at local levels, often to ill effect. And China's people are still relocating en masse, sometimes forcibly, as in the case of the millions moved for the Three Gorges Dam, sometimes voluntarily. . . . Less obviously, but also significantly, China's environmental problems are linked to the ideological bankruptcy and disillusionment left by the country's Maoist experiment. (Shapiro 2001, 203)

All else being equal, most Chinese would probably want to buy cleaner automobiles to contribute to cleaner air. Who actually desires more air pollution? But, of course, all else is not equal, and the strength of the demand for cleaner and more efficient automobiles depends on the commitment and power of those asking for such technologies and the competing demands and so-called opportunity costs. The Chinese government has asserted that environmental protection is a real priority for China, it has passed laws on air and water pollution, and it is working to improve enforcement of these laws. China has also actively engaged in international negotiations for multilateral environmental agreements (MEAs). In 1999, China hosted its first United Nations–sponsored meeting on environmental protection, the Eleventh Meeting of the Parties to the Montreal Protocol on Substances That Deplete the Ozone Layer. President Jiang Zemin personally came to the meeting at the Beijing International Convention Center to address the delegates. He stated:

The Chinese government has always attached great importance to environmental protection. China regards environmental protection as a basic state policy, has adopted the strategy of sustainable development, has undertaken effective measures for pollution prevention and control and ecological conservation, and has promoted the coordinated development of economy and environment. . . . As a developing country, China is willing to bear the international responsibilities and obligations appropriate to its level of development on a fair, just, and reasonable basis, and make its contribution to the promotion of global environment and development. (Jiang 1999).

Currently, provincial governments own most of the major automobile firms, and the most powerful central government ministries are the ones most concerned with economic development and growth. At the same time, the Chinese government controls the GONGOs. The true desires of the Chinese citizenry are thus masked behind government ownership and organization. The only way that Chinese people can express their preferences is through the market. If they demand cleaner vehicles in the marketplace, Chinese automobile producers may be forced to respond.

A Vicious Circle or Marriage of Convenience?

The possible existence of either a "vicious circle" or a "marriage of convenience" is the fourth explanation for why U.S. firms did not transfer cleaner technologies to China. This helps to explain why the Chinese government has not regulated the Sino-U.S. joint-venture firms more aggressively. In an interview, one Chinese official of the State Environmental Protection Agency (SEPA) described a vicious circle in the Chinese government's decision-making process that has to do with domestic competitiveness. Chinese environmental law treats both domestic and foreign-invested joint-venture auto companies the same. The Chinese government is reluctant to add additional burdens to the struggles of Chinese companies by imposing laws with which they could not easily comply. The Chinese domestic firms lack the advanced environmental technologies, so the Chinese government holds back from imposing stiffer environmental standards even on the Sino-foreign joint ventures, although it would be relatively easy and cheap for the foreign-affiliated joint venture arms to comply. Without the government's requiring the foreign firms to transfer cleaner technologies through more aggressive regulations, Chinese firms cannot access the technology through the technology-transfer process. Since Chinese firms still do not have the capability to design the cleaner technologies themselves, they fall even further behind the foreigners. Their ever-increasing backwardness makes it even more difficult for the Chinese government to risk imposing more stringent standards, and the downward spiral continues. A U.S. employee of one of the joint-venture companies made the same observation. He said, "The Chinese government doesn't want to penalize the Chinese companies, especially the small ones, so it is slow to require changes of all the companies." Moreover, "If the government put policies in place to require advanced technologies, the Chinese companies/engineers would somehow do it. And, certainly, the foreign companies would transfer the technologies" (interview with E. Clark, Beijing, 2002).

A more cynical view of this dynamic is that, instead of a vicious circle being the culprit, it could just be a marriage of convenience between the foreign-funded joint-venture firms and the Chinese government. The government knows that restructuring China's domestic automobile industry will be very painful and difficult, so it keeps delaying the inevitable by moving slowly on environmental regulations despite rhetoric to the contrary in the auto-industry policies. Meanwhile, the foreign-affiliated joint ventures are not exactly demanding that the Chinese government impose more stringent pollution-control laws (nor are they imposing more stringent internal standards for their own operations in China). So everyone lives with the status quo, but human health and environmental quality in China suffer.

There are two ways to break the vicious circle. One is to improve and develop domestic technological capabilities for these cleaner technologies within the Chinese firms. This is exactly what the Ministry of Science and Technology (MOST) is trying to do through its relatively new high-tech research program on clean vehicles. The main problem with this program is that MOST has decided to try to leapfrog over all conventional automotive technologies by only investing in component technology for electric, hybrid-electric, and fuel-cell vehicles without any accompanying policies to push these technologies into the marketplace. The other way to break the vicious circle is for the Chinese government simply to issue the regulations and accept that some domestic Chinese firms may suffer or be forced to consolidate. Either way, such steps would actually be in accordance with the Chinese government's goals for the industry, because the government would like to consolidate China's auto firms into six big companies akin to the "Big Three" structure in the United States (State Economic and Trade Commission of China 2001). Stringent performance standards would force the foreigners to transfer more advanced technology and enable the Chinese firms to demand cleaner technology when they bargain with their foreign partner. If the joint ventures called for higher standards, they could indirectly drive their domestic competitors out of business, and this might be a method of generating a virtuous circle of better environmental standards and increased FDI. The fact that the joint ventures have not called for more stringent environmental standards supports the "marriage of convenience" hypothesis, and it also reveals that the domestic producers are not real sources of competition either.

Poor Fuel Quality

The fifth and final reason why outdated technologies for automotive air-pollution control have been transferred to China has to do with one important physical constraint: China's poor fuel quality. Recently, China phased out leaded fuel in less than five years, which was an impressive achievement. The sulfur levels of most Chinese petroleum products, however, remain high. A high sulfur level in gasoline limits the ability of catalytic converters in automobiles to lower CO, HC, and NO_x emissions. China's crude oil is characterized as "heavy, low-sulfur and waxy," but most of China's imported crude is high in sulfur. The resulting sulfur level of refined gasoline available in China is currently about 800 ppm for gasoline. In Europe, gasoline sulfur levels were set at 500 ppm for their EURO II fuel standard, 150 ppm for EURO III, and 50 ppm for EURO IV (Walsh 2003).

U.S. firms often cite the high sulfur levels in Chinese fuels as a barrier to deployment of cleaner automotive technologies. They argue that sulfur levels are so high that even if U.S. firms did transfer cleaner automotive technologies, their effectiveness would be muted, or even undermined, by poor fuel quality. For example, GM believes that it would be very difficult to meet EURO III emission standards without an improvement in the fuels (interview with P. Murtaugh, chair and CEO, China Group, General Motors China, Shanghai, 2002). Why sulfur levels remain so high in Chinese fuels is not the subject of this study, but suffice to say that it would be expensive for China to lower the sulfur levels in its fuels because all of its refineries would need major investments to upgrade to cleaner fuels. As of 2005, refineries were not permitted to set the price of refined products like gasoline, so they could not pass on the costs of such upgrades even if they wanted to make these upgrades.

Why Technology Transfer Is Not Improving Environmental Quality in China

To some extent, U.S. foreign direct investment helped to deploy cleaner automotive technologies in China than those that were in use before due to the introduction of more modern technologies such as electronic fuel-injection engines, but the potential environmental benefit of the newer technologies is being offset by the huge growth in the number of cars on the road. There is some variation among the three U.S. firms in terms of how much cleaner the technologies transferred actually were. This variation can most readily be explained by differences in Chinese policy at the time each joint venture was negotiated. When the Chinese government issued policies that created strong incentives for technology transfer, more modern (and therefore, somewhat cleaner) products were transferred. Also, when the Chinese government issued air-pollution-control regulations, all three U.S. firms readily worked with their Chinese partners to comply.

The Scale Effect

Trade liberalization and foreign direct investment can have three effects on the environment of a recipient country: technique, scale, and composition (Grossman and Kruger 1991, 3–5):

First, there is the *scale* effect. . . . That is, if trade and investment liberalization cause an expansion of economic activity, and if the nature of that activity remains unchanged, then the total amount of pollution generated must increase. . . .

Second, there is a *composition* effect. . . . If competitive advantage derives largely from differences in environmental regulation then the composition effect of trade liberalization will be damaging to the environment. Each country then will tend to specialize more completely in the activities that its government does not regulate directly, and will shift out of production in industries where the local costs of pollution abatement are relatively great. . . .

Finally, there is a *technique* effect. That is, output need not be produced by exactly the same methods subsequent to a liberalization of trade and foreign investment as it had been prior to the change in the regime. In particular, the output of pollution per unit of economic product need not remain the same. There are at least two reasons to believe that pollution per unit of output might fall, especially in a less developed country. First, foreign producers might transfer modern technologies to the local economy when restrictions on foreign investment are relaxed. More modern technologies typically are cleaner than older technologies due to the growing awareness of the urgency of environmental concerns. Second, and perhaps more importantly, if trade liberalization generates an increase in income levels, then the body politic may demand a cleaner environment as an expression of their increased national wealth. Thus, more stringent pollution standards and stricter enforcement of existing laws may be a natural political response to economic growth.[2]

In the case of U.S. foreign direct investment in China's automobile industry, the small technique effect from the slightly cleaner pollution-control technologies is being offset by the huge scale effect of the tremendous growth in the sales of new automobiles.

Even though U.S. and other foreign firms introduced slightly more modern (but hardly state-of-the-art) pollution-control technologies to China, the potential benefit in terms of air-pollution reductions has been vastly outstripped by the increased air pollution caused by the rapid growth in the production and sales in the Chinese automobile industry. It is not possible to measure exactly how *much* cleaner the transferred technologies were in comparison with the domestic technologies because no data were collected. But, once the Chinese government imposed its EURO I automotive emission standard, U.S. firms immediately transferred the pollution-control technologies required to meet this standard to their joint-venture partners in China. Before the standard was issued, however, Beijing Jeep did not transfer the pollution-control technology (GM and Ford's production began after they knew the EURO I regulations were scheduled to take effect in 2000).

Although it cannot be exactly measured, it is clear that the "scale" effect has so far been large in China; indeed, during the last decade, motor vehicles became significant sources of urban air pollution in China. Air pollution from all sources (including automobiles) is estimated to cause 300,000 Chinese citizens to die prematurely each year (Economy 1999). During the 1990s, the total number of passenger cars produced in China grew tenfold, from less than 100,000 per year in 1991 to more than 1 million in 2002. Such dramatic growth explains why total emissions of certain air pollutants from passenger vehicles have sharply increased even as somewhat cleaner technology from U.S. and other foreign firms was introduced into China.

Barriers and Incentives

Barriers and incentives for technology transfer tend to be fairly specific to a particular circumstance (Reddy 1996). It has proven difficult for analysts to determine which ones are generally most significant, and especially which ones matter the most for "sustainable" or "clean" technology transfer (Metz, Davidson, et al. 2000).[3] There is general agreement that special barriers and incentives for environmental technology transfer do exist, but paradoxically, one of the most recent and comprehensive studies of the transfer of sustainable technology concludes that "there are *no* corresponding overarching theories" about environmentally sound technology transfer, only a "number of pathways" (Metz, Davidson, et al. 2000). This Intergovernmental Panel on Climate Change (IPCC) study concludes that the "pathway" is determined by the role of the key stakeholder. These three main pathways are: government-driven, private sector-driven, and community-driven.

Thus, the incentives and barriers to sustainable technology transfer depend on who is participating in the process (Trindade, Siddiqi, and Martinot 2000). So while there may be no "theory" of sustainable-technology transfer, generalizations have again been formed about how such technology is usually transferred, what barriers exist, and how those barriers could be overcome. Empirical studies are beginning to show on a case-by-case basis which barriers and incentives are the most important in environmentally related technology transfer (Ohshita and Ortolano 2002).

To focus explicitly on cleaner-*energy*-technology transfer, Martinot, Sinton, and Haddad (1997) propose a useful framework. They argue there are three useful perspectives for examining the process of energy-technology transfer from industrialized to developing countries:

- Technological
- Market/transaction (economic costs and benefits)
- Agent/agenda perspectives

Technological perspectives highlight technology needs, choices, and development. A market/transaction approach highlights the importance of the technology's price or cost, the evolution of markets, and the types of institutions and transactions that underlie them. The agent/agenda viewpoint highlights the different types of actors who can influence technology transfer (Martinot, Sinton, and Haddad 1997). There are two weaknesses in this framework: key barriers and incentives might be obscured by only delineating three main perspectives, and the relative importance of each factor is not expressed. In the 2000 IPCC study on Methodological and Technological Issues in Technology Transfer, no fewer than twenty-two barriers were identified for what the authors call "environmentally-sound" technology transfer (see table 8.4). Even so, by just glancing at this list, one can see that many of these barriers are not necessarily unique to environmentally sound technology transfer. Other barriers seem more distinctive, such as the lack of full-cost pricing, which would incorporate the costs to society of environmental damage. A similar list could be generated for the incentives for technology transfer, and the IPCC provides one chapter on what it calls "enabling environments." These environments generally encourage the development of national systems of innovation, participatory approaches, building institutions (forming codes, standards, and certification procedures), building human and institutional capacities, and stimulating R&D activities. By examining the cases of technology transfer from the United States to China in the automobile industry, the specific barriers that are most inhibitory to cleaner-technology transfer in the Chinese automobile industry, and the incentives most likely to facilitate cleaner-technology transfer, have been identified in this chapter.[4]

Many other barriers are commonly cited in the literature for why it is generally difficult to transfer technologies from advanced-idustrial countries to developing countries, such as concerns about intellectual property rights, competition, poor communication, lack of supporting infrastructure, unrealistic expectations, cultural differences, and the

Table 8.4
Barriers to the transfer of environmentally sound technologies (ESTs)

Lack of full-cost pricing
Poor macroeconomic conditions (i.e., underdeveloped financial sector, high import duties)
Low private-sector involvement because of lack of access to capital
Lack of financial institutions or systems to ensure initial investments for the use of transferred technologies
Conventional energy prices are low (and are often subsidized), resulting in negative incentives to adopt energy-saving measures and renewable-energy technologies
Lack of markets for ESTs
Lack of supporting legal institutions and frameworks, including codes and standards for the evaluation and implementation of ESTs
Lack of understanding of the role of developed and developing countries and international institutions in the failures and successes of past technology cooperation
Lack of support for an open and transparent international banking and trading system
Corruption
Reluctance to identify and make available ESTs that are in the public domain
Insufficient human and institutional capabilities
Inadequate vision about and understanding of local needs and demands
Inadequate capacity to assess, select, import, develop, and adapt appropriate technologies
Lack of confidence in unproven technologies
Lack of data, information, knowledge, and awareness of "emerging" technologies
Lack of confidence in unproven technology
Risk aversion and practices that favor large projects in financial institutions, including multilateral development banks
Insufficient R&D
Inadequate resources for project implementation
High transaction costs
Lack of access to relevant, credible, and timely information on potential partners, which could enhance the spread of ESTs

Source: Excerpted from Metz et al. IPCC, *Methodological and Technological Issues in Technology Transfer*, 2000.

appropriateness of technologies for the recipient country (Reddy 1996; Guerin 2001). Such analysis is not very helpful because technology transfer is so dependent on the particular context in which it occurs. In a 1990 study of U.S.-China technology transfer, the three most important barriers that were identified were effective communication, surrounding infrastructure, and decision-making processes in China (Schnepp, von Glinow, and Bhambri 1990). In the three specific cases of Shanghai GM, Chang'An Ford, and Beijing Jeep, U.S. firms dismissed all such barriers as mere business challenges that had been readily overcome with effort, determination, and creativity. The complexity of the technology-transfer process itself is another barrier that seems compelling, but there was no evidence that any of the joint ventures had trouble with the actual process of transferring technology.

The two most effective incentives identified by this book for the deployment of cleaner automotive technology through technology transfer are: (1) Chinese policies that set performance standards for automobiles; and (2) market competition. These findings support the results of another study that concluded that "whether a country imports equipment to lower pollution depends upon the strength of environmental regulations"(Lanjouw and Mody 1996, 566).[5] When the Chinese government issued its first emission-control policy in 2000, U.S. firms immediately responded by transferring the requisite emission-control technologies to their joint ventures in China. The increasing market competition during the late 1990s, initially sparked by GM's introduction of the Buick New Century sedan (and later China's entry into the WTO), provoked the introduction of many relatively modern automobile technologies (such as the VW Passat, VW Polo, and the Toyota Xiali 2000). As GM China's CEO remarked, "Shanghai GM had to both improve its product and lower the price a little because of increased competition" (interview with P. Murtaugh, Shanghai, 2002).

9
Technology Transfer, Innovation, and Economic Development

Technology transfer from foreign companies enabled a complete transformation of China's automobile industry during the 1980s and 1990s. The Chinese industry went from producing a total of less than 100,000 passenger cars annually before 1990 to producing millions just a decade later. Such vast expansion in output brought along many benefits for the rest of the economy, from providing a demand for energy and other materials like steel and rubber, to creating and sustaining large numbers of jobs for Chinese citizens. Without the technology transfer from foreign firms, it is virtually impossible that the Chinese firms would have been able to achieve these gains alone.

The main finding with respect to technology transfer and economic development that emerges from analyzing the three U.S.-China joint-venture firms is that while the U.S. firms were effective at getting foreign models into production in China (and improving Chinese manufacturing capabilities in the process), U.S. foreign direct investment did not strongly contribute to improving Chinese innovation capabilities in the automotive sector because little knowledge beyond how to manufacture was transferred along with the product. The failure thus far of the Chinese firms to learn how to design and produce vehicles themselves through the technology-transfer process can be mainly attributed to a lack of initiative and creativity on their part to learn more from their foreign partners. The foreign companies have viewed their Chinese counterparts primarily as manufacturing and assembly partners, not strategic partners for the long term, because otherwise they would have invested more in strengthening Chinese technological capabilities so that they could contribute to product development and innovation. This indicates that the U.S. and other foreign firms are afraid of spawning competitors and that there is still a lack of trust and true partnership between the U.S. and Chinese firms.

In this chapter, the extent of technological cooperation among the three joint ventures will be assessed before exploring the role of technology transfer in the economic development of the Chinese automobile industry.

Technology Cooperation

As of 2002, the three joint ventures varied considerably in terms of the extent of their technological cooperation (see table 9.1). Two of the three joint ventures had established some form of a technical center, but none of the Sino-foreign joint ventures actually did fundamental research and experimentation together. In every joint venture, the U.S. and Chinese partners were working together on product adaptation as well as localization of parts and components. Beijing Jeep and Chang'An Ford's technical personnel were internal to their joint ventures. At Beijing Jeep, the technical center was entirely staffed by Chinese engineers and codirected by one Chinese and one U.S. manager. Shanghai GM opted to establish a separate joint venture for its technical center, the Pan Asia Technical Automotive Center (PATAC). This center was not explicitly tied to Shanghai GM, although 80 percent of its work was contracted by SGM. PATAC helped to adapt the Opel Corsa to the Chinese market in its reincarnation as the Buick Sail (interview in Detroit with C. Green, executive director, Regional Science and Technology, General Motors Asia Pacific Ltd., 2002). U.S. and Chinese engineers jointly managed PATAC, although there was a ratio of twenty Chinese engineers for every one U.S. engineer. U.S. engineers managed seven of the eleven major departments at PATAC. The Chinese managers ran the human resources, marketing, purchasing, and testing departments. U.S. managers ran the body, chassis, powertrain, interior design, electrical, and HVAC divisions (interview with GM China Chinese employee B, Shanghai, 2002).

Although none of the technical centers was doing R&D internally as of 2002, this circumstance does not mean that the U.S. firms were not investing in R&D in China. To the contrary, both GM and Ford were investing in research projects, but not with their joint-venture partners

Table 9.1

Comparative analysis of technological cooperation as of 2002

	Beijing Jeep	Shanghai GM	Chang'An Ford
Technology center?	Yes, internal	Yes (PATAC)	No
Capability level of Chinese partner according to U.S. firm	Product adaptation, localization	Product adaptation, localization	
Does U.S. firm fund other research in Chinese universities or institutes?	No	Yes, total of US$1.97 million from 6/96 to 12/02. About US$20,000–$30,000 per project per year. 100% is applied research.	Yes—total amount not disclosed. The program is coordinated with the National Science Foundation of China
Number of Chinese vs. U.S. engineers Management of technical centers	200 Chinese, 1 U.S. 1 Chinese, 1 U.S.	400 Chinese, >20 U.S. 7 of 11 major departments managed by U.S. engineers	
Funding	n/a	For PATAC, GM put US$25 million in cash and SAIC put US$22 million in kind	n/a

in China. Both firms were investing in Chinese universities and academic institutes. From 1996 to 2002, GM had invested a total of US$1.97 million in different projects at a number of top Chinese universities (interview with C. Green, Detroit, 2002). GM did a study to determine which universities possessed the best capabilities, and it distributed about US$20,000–$30,000 for each project to these top universities at the time. U.S. firms were already noting the cost advantage of Chinese researchers. The former executive director of Regional Science and Technology for GM Asia Pacific commented that GM had estimated that for "time on target" (time purely devoted to the research project), Tsinghua University researchers cost "one-fifth" as much as U.S. university researchers. But Chinese university researchers are only being funded to do applied research projects, not basic research. According to Green, "GM funds no basic science in China." So there already appears to be an emerging cost advantage to funding applied R&D projects in China, and this is especially significant because GM's overall research budget is proportioned heavily in favor of applied R&D (80 percent). Thus, Chinese university researchers could increasingly supplant U.S.-based researchers. Green said that in the future, projects would be chosen in Asia "based on cost, quality, and geographic clustering" (interview with C. Green, Detroit, 2002).

Ford China has also chosen to invest directly in Chinese universities and institutes, without channeling this investment through its joint venture. This investment has been done in coordination with the National Science Foundation of China. The director of International Research and Technology, Asia Pacific, South America, and South Africa for Ford Research Laboratory declined to be interviewed for this study, so further comparative analysis is not possible.

Beijing Jeep had not chosen to invest in research in China as of 2002. To some extent, however, DaimlerChrysler was investing in product development and adaptation for localization purposes. According to one DaimlerChrysler manager, "For high-end premium SUVs with relatively small volume niches, it would be a definite challenge for the manufacturer to invest heavily in research and development in localizing high content levels of both parts and components. We must have enough market volume (in China) to justify high local content of parts and components" (interview with W.-M. Soh, vice president, Special Project, BJC Sales and Marketing, DaimlerChrysler, Beijing, 2002).

To underline the point made above, none of the U.S. firms were actually funding automotive R&D projects within their own manufacturing joint venture as of 2002. Instead, the companies were choosing to fund research projects at Chinese universities. This finding implies that Chinese technological capabilities are better in the universities than in the Chinese automotive firms, and it raises interesting questions about China's national automotive-innovation system. If the best technological capabilities reside in the universities, what is the connection between the Chinese universities and Chinese firms? Anecdotally, there was little evidence for substantial interaction between the firms and universities, but this question is ripe for future research.

Stagnation and Technological Lock-In

Part of the promise of foreign direct investment is that it brings modern technologies to the recipient country. One would expect that as improved technologies became available, foreign joint-venture partners would transfer them to China. And, as better environmental technologies were developed, they too would be transferred. In the cases of foreign automobile firms operating in China, vehicle models were not necessarily updated in tandem with updates to equivalent foreign models during the 1980s and 1990s.[1] An important implication of this finding is that the Chinese auto industry essentially "locked in" to outdated, inefficient, and polluting vehicle technologies for many years, until a combination of increased competition and new government policies provoked the introduction of newer and cleaner technologies in the late 1990s. Although automobiles have a relatively short lifetime compared with other energy technologies such as power plants, if the same technology is in production for a decade or more, then the entire model fleet on the road operates with old technologies—essentially locked into a dated technological system. Such lock-in creates persistent market and policy failures that can inhibit the diffusion of cleaner technologies (Unruh 2000). In terms of automobiles, China got stuck with older technologies that were somewhat path-dependent, and they inhibited the diffusion of cleaner technologies, as discussed in the vicious-circle section of the previous chapter.

Several case studies of technology transfer from foreign firms to China's offshore oil industry were conducted in the early 1990s. In cases of successful technology transfer,

The adoption of a new technology did not mark the end of the technology transfer process, but rather for the full benefit of an innovation to be realized, technology was continually changed and improved. The learning process arising from such activities was shown to be improved when suppliers and recipients worked together to modify the technology to suit new problems and conditions. (Warhurst 1991, 1070)

Based on this experience, it can be inferred that when there is no process of continually changing and improving technologies once they are in production, technology transfer is less successful because there are fewer opportunities for the two partners to learn from each other.

With the model updates at Shanghai GM in the late 1990s, and the new Beijing Jeep 2500 Cherokee model introduced in May 2003, one can observe a change for the better in recent years. Initially, the concept of "new model years" was not transferred to China along with the initial automotive technologies. Instead, once a model was put into production in China, it remained in production virtually unchanged for decades. If the model became obsolete, the foreign firm would usually introduce a completely new model rather than improve the technology of the existing model in production.

There are six main reasons for the stagnation of the automotive technology transfer through 2002 (as listed in table 9.2): first, the cost of updating technologies that were already localized in China was high; second, production volumes were very low for many years, so it was hard to recover the initial capital investment in the manufacturing technology; third, the lack of market competition provided few incentives for updating technology until the late 1990s; fourth, there were no clear policy mandates to update the technology; fifth, there was limited consumer demand in earlier years; and sixth, the same "good-enough phe-

Table 9.2
Technological stagnation from 1984 to 2002

Explanation	Beijing Jeep	Shanghai GM	Chang'An Ford
Cost of updating localized technologies	✓		n/a
Low production volume	✓		n/a
Lack of market competition	✓		n/a
Lack of policy mandate	✓	✓	✓
Lack of consumer demand	✓		n/a
The "good-enough" phenomenon	✓		n/a

Note: Production at Chang'An Ford began in early 2003, so it is not possible to analyze its performance in this respect as of this date.

nomenon" (described in chapter 8) applies to this finding. Again, there was variation among the three cases in this regard.

The Jeep Cherokee was the first foreign model to be manufactured by a joint-venture company in China. The Cherokee was introduced in 1985 and it was a current model at that time. The Cherokee was initially assembled from complete knockdown kits (CKDs) sent from Detroit. Over time, many of the parts were localized, in part motivated by the 1994 Auto Industry Policy requiring a minimum of 40 percent of parts to be produced by Chinese manufacturers. The Cherokee that was still in production at Beijing Jeep (until being replaced by the new Cherokee Jeep 2500 in 2003) had experienced some updates since 1984, such as brake improvements, distributorless engines, and the installation of electronic fuel injection in the automobiles.[2] No Cherokee model is still produced in the United States (it was replaced by the Jeep Liberty model). During the mid-1990s, the Cherokee engine, transmission, and suspension were installed in the old BJ2020 model, and that was the full extent of "refreshing" that the BJ2020 ever received from AMC or Chrysler. This situation proved to be a profitable arrangement.

According to a DaimlerChrysler manager, "In a normal circumstance, a manufacturer will launch an entirely new model every five to seven years and a 'refresh' (face-lift) every 1.5 years, but BJC did not do that in the period 1984–2002 with the Jeep Cherokee" (interview with W.-M. Soh, Beijing, 2002). At the end of 2002, however, Beijing Jeep finally decided to refresh the Jeep Cherokee by introducing a new model in 2003, the Jeep 2500. Soh promised that for the Grand Cherokee, Mitsubishi Pajaro, and others, Beijing Jeep intended to carry out "respective timetables in launching new models and also refreshing all products from 2002 onward."

Until the 1990s, Beijing Jeep faced little competition. Initially, the biggest market for its automobiles was the Chinese military, which had a standing order for a certain number of Jeeps per year. BJC had essentially no competition in this market, which was not really a market at all because the government specified how many Jeeps should be produced for the military each year. The only other foreign joint venture established in China during the mid-1980s was Volkswagen's joint venture with SAIC, signed in 1984.[3] Shanghai VW and Beijing Jeep produced very different products. The first model produced by Shanghai VW was the midsized Santana sedan, primarily sold in the Shanghai market for use as taxis. The Shanghai government provided market protection for Shanghai VW by mandating that all taxis must have engines of a certain size, conveniently the size of the Santana engine. From the start, there was weak consumer demand for the Cherokee as a passenger car. Government officials preferred to be chauffeured in a sedan, and Cherokees were not used as taxis. Thus, the Cherokee was simply not viewed as a passenger car by the two biggest categories of Chinese consumers at the time.

Because there was relatively little demand for the Jeeps, production volumes remained low, and this volume made it difficult to justify modernizing the vehicles. Beijing Jeep achieved its peak production in 1995 when 50,000 BJ2020s and 30,000 Cherokees were sold, but by 2002 production had fallen sharply to only 10,000 vehicles for all models. Once it became clear that the Cherokee was not selling well, Chrysler decided to introduce the Grand Cherokee. The Grand Cherokee was introduced in 2001 and it has not sold well either. The following rationale for this failure was provided by the company:

One of the problems with the Grand Cherokee is that it is a high-tech and complex machine. The Jeep Cherokee is relatively much more simple and therefore easy for mechanics to handle. The Jeep Grand Cherokee is so computerized that the mechanics need a lot of training. This is why an after-sales network is so important. Thus sales volume on the Jeep Grand Cherokee will increase in conjunction with the establishment of the 3S dealer network facility in China. (interview with W.-M. Soh, Beijing, 2002)

The Shanghai GM and Chang'An Ford cases are quite different. Shanghai GM did make a number of technical changes to its New Century luxury sedan once it was in production, including reducing the size of the engine to improve fuel economy, reducing noise levels, and upgrading the interior. Chang'An Ford only started production in February 2003, so it is too soon to evaluate this joint venture in this respect. By one Ford employee's account, Ford probably could have done more in terms of the level of technology transferred. Still, all Shanghai GM and Chang'An Ford vehicles meet the same EURO II standard required in China's biggest cities, so it is likely that the environmental effect of the technology transfer is about the same.

Technology Transfer, FDI, and Economic Development

It is worth exploring the contexts of international technology transfer with respect to economic development. One of the biggest theoretical benefits of foreign direct investment is that technology transfer will accompany it. In the cases of U.S. FDI into China's automobile industry, technology transfer must be understood to occur within a much broader context: international policies and institutions, globalization, U.S.-China bilateral relations, and domestic industrial and environmental policies are all interactions that will bear on how or why technology is transferred. International policies and institutions may establish norms, rules, and guidelines that can affect technology transfer. For example, the Multilateral Agreement on Investment (MAI) that was proposed by the OECD (but never enacted) would have established international rules for foreign investment. Forces of globalization are creating pressure for lower trade barriers and greater access to global markets. Bilateral foreign relations between the United States and China can obviously create conditions for greater or less cooperation between their citizens and private firms. Currently, technology transfer between the United States and China in the auto industry is fundamentally a process of U.S. technology innovation and subsequent transfer of marketable technologies to China, primarily through the private sector. Domestic policies in both countries will therefore also affect the choice and degree of technologies transferred.

Technology Transfer as Part of the Innovation Process

Theoretically, technology transfer must be considered in the context of the technological innovation process. A number of stylized models of the innovation process have been proposed and refined during the last century. Initially, these models conceived of innovation as a linear and sequential process, which began with research, proceeded to development, then to demonstration, and finally to production and deployment.[4] Later, this theoretical model was refined to capture two-way or iterative "chain-linked" interactions where learning in one phase was linked to the other phases (Kline and Rosenberg 1986). A third model proposed by Ken-ichi Imai described the Japanese practice of merging the research, development, demonstration, and deployment (RD³) phases so that there is substantial overlap between the stages. In this last formulation, none of the stages occurs in isolation and the more the stages overlap with each other, the more efficient the "integrated" innovation process (Brooks 1995). Thus, technology innovation is characterized by multiple dynamic feedbacks (Grubler 1998). Conceptually, technology transfer occurs in the realm of technology deployment or diffusion. Diffusion is "the process by which an innovation is communicated through certain channels over time among the members of a social system" (Rogers 1995, 5). Some argue that there is little that is unique about the process of technology transfer to distinguish it from technology deployment in general (Brooks 1995). If this is true, one can explore the theories about technological diffusion as they might apply to technology transfer.

Little has been proven definitively about the causes of technology deployment, but two general descriptive models exist: the S-curve or life-cycle model and the learning/experience-curve model. In the life-cycle model, the diffusion and growth of a technology often proceeds along an S-shaped or logistic curve: slow growth of technology diffusion at the beginning, followed by accelerating growth that eventually slows when the market is saturated. This model illuminates the point that the rate of technology deployment is often nonlinear for some time before reaching a limit or saturation. The learning-curve model shows that the unit costs of production often decrease as experience producing the product output increases. But the rate of learning can vary enormously among different sectors and technologies (Grubler 1998; McDonald and Schrattenholzer 2001), and the rate may undergo sudden, discontinuous changes as specific innovations are introduced.[5]

Technology Acquisition, Learning, and Economic Development

There has been considerable debate about the importance of technology transfer and technological diffusion to economic development. The classic Heckscher-Ohlin theory of trade assumed that technology did not play a determining role in defining a nation's comparative advantage.[6] Indeed, this theory attributes comparative advantage only to the relative difference in capital and labor-factor abundance between trading partners. Trading on this basis, they postulated, can result in gains from trade and subsequent economic development. Technology was assumed to be equal across nations because it was considered well defined, free, and perfectly available.

In his *Theory of Economic Development*, Joseph Schumpeter proposed an alternative theory of economic development, which explicitly hypothesized the centrality of technological change to economic development. Schumpeter wrote that "new combinations" (in other words, technical change) can be considered a factor of production, and that these new combinations "do not fall from heaven," but are "created . . . by the individual waves of development." For Schumpeter, "The phenomenon characterizing development emerges" when "new combinations appear discontinuously" (Schumpeter 1934, 66). In other words, technological change is intrinsic to economic development, but it is not an automatic process.[7]

The idea that technology was equally available across nations endured in the economic-development literature for decades after Schumpeter proposed otherwise.[8] But increasingly, economists began to accumulate evidence that economic output cannot be explained by labor and capital alone. Robert M. Solow and others showed that there is a "residual" that must be technology's contribution to economic growth (Solow 1957; Griliches 1996). Thus, technology is now considered essential to economic development along with labor and capital.

Although possession of technology is necessary for economic output, it is hard to acquire. Many empirical studies have shown that technology is tacit, proprietary, and often expensive. These studies show that the acquisition of technology in late-industrializing economies is a complex process because of these characteristics of technology. Successful acquisition of technology usually requires, among other things, active government involvement and management, selectivity and planning with respect to which technologies to acquire (and in what order), determination and skill on the part of the recipient firm, and specific contractual arrangements between buyer and seller (Dahlman, Ross-Larson, and Westphal 1987; Amsden 1989, 2001; Warhurst 1991; Reddy 1996; Kim and Nelson 2000; Lall 2000).

Although it is difficult to acquire advanced technology for the purposes of furthering economic development, overcoming these difficulties is essential for accelerating the development process of many industrializing countries, including that of China. This study of technology transfer from the United States to China in the automobile industry adds additional empirical evidence to the accumulating body of literature on the difficulties related to transferring technology to industrializing countries. It also highlights the need for governments and firms in these countries to work strategically to acquire advanced technological capabilities to succeed in a knowledge-based global economy.

A number of barriers to economically efficient technology diffusion in an industrializing country have been identified, including the existence of transaction costs (North 1965), market failures such as imperfect information (Stiglitz 1989), the proprietary nature of technology (Hymer 1976), and the problem that technology is tacit (not outright or explicit). A firm is a bundle of proprietary assets, and these assets include technological capabilities and skills (Amsden 2001). Other barriers include the recipient or buyer's capacity to absorb technology, the importance of being able to learn by doing, the appropriateness of the technology to its new setting, the costs of the advanced technologies for both acquisition and deployment, indigenous technological capabilities, and uncertainty (Arrow 1962; Baranson and Roark 1985; Dahlman, Ross-Larson, and Westphal 1987; Yin 1992; B. Xu 2000; Ohshita and Ortolano 2002). Finally, *access* to technology cannot be automatically equated with improved technological *capabilities* that can contribute to economic growth (Reddy and Zhao 1990).[9] All of these market "failures" imply a need for government intervention, in so far as policies and regulations can create incentives for and eliminate barriers to the effective acquisition, absorption, and deployment of technology through technology transfer. One cross-sector study of technology transfer to China noted that "government plays a critical role in the process of indigenizing foreign technology" (Yin 1992).

In terms of incentives for technology diffusion, policy and economic-competitiveness factors seem to provide the strongest incentives to firms. For example, new regulations and laws, along with increased market competition in the recipient country, can affect the process of technology transfer and diffusion. In one study of the Chinese steel industry, it was found that larger and younger firms were more likely to adopt energy-saving, continuous-casting technologies, and that the availability of investment, higher profit rates, and local ownership also accelerated the diffusion of continuous-casting technology (Fisher-Vanden 2003). There can also be ethical, political, environmental, and diplomatic motivations for technology transfer and diffusion.

The Relationships among FDI, Technology Transfer, and Economic Development

The promise of foreign direct investment has been considerable. FDI is considered by many to be a strong contributor to economic growth and industrial development because it provides financing for worthy projects and can serve as an effective mechanism for technology transfer (OECD 2002). Along with the technology transfer, proponents expect that FDI will cause integration with the world economy, backward and forward linkages to related industries (spillovers), human-capital formation, and surges in domestic innovation.[10] Increasingly, this promise is being challenged by empirical evidence that FDI does not automatically provide these benefits to developing countries. FDI does not always accelerate growth, generate linkages and spillovers, and provoke greater innovation (Saggi 2002). In fact, there is evidence that FDI can correlate negatively with some indicators of innovation: the more FDI, the less industrial innovation on the part of the developing economy (Amsden 2001). Lastly, it has been shown that when conceived as "cumulative learning," technology transfer does not automatically occur through FDI (Saggi 2002).

There are other potential downsides associated with FDI: it can be associated with greater environmental degradation, labor abuses in the supply chain, increased inequality, deterioration of the balance of payments, increased financial volatility, and the crowding out of domestic companies (OECD 2002). The extent to which FDI produces positive benefits is strongly dependent on the particular context in which the investment is made. If there are good policies, effective institutions, motivated recipient firms, and "enlightened" foreign firms, FDI is more likely to have a positive effect on the local economy.

No single international institution governs foreign direct investment by transnational corporations.[11] During the mid-1990s, the Organization for Economic Cooperation and Development (OECD) initiated a discussion among its members about creating a Multilateral Agreement on

Investment (MAI). The initial framework of the MAI was perceived to be strongly tilted toward the interests of the foreign investor rather than the needs and interests of the recipient. Also, the MAI did not have substantive protections for labor and the environment. After much criticism, the MAI was abandoned and replaced in 2000 by an updated set of voluntary guidelines called the OECD Guidelines for Multinational Enterprises. These guidelines provide voluntary principles and standards for "responsible business conduct," in a variety of areas including employment and industrial relations, human rights, bribery, disclosure, environment, information disclosure, competition, taxation, and science and technology" (OECD 2000, 5).[12] Many developing countries have some rules associated with the inflow of FDI, but these rules vary widely.

China receives more foreign direct investment than any other developing nation and has consistently done so since the mid-1990s.[13] Within China, the automobile industry has received a huge proportion of total FDI; for example, GM's investment represented the largest single foreign investment ever made in China. At the beginning of 2001, it was estimated that more than 800 Chinese companies in related industries had received FDI during the past decade, with US$12 billion of investment actually registered in China (Zhang 2002). The question to be answered next is whether effective technology transfer accompanied this abundance of FDI in China's auto industry.

FDI and Chinese Innovation Capabilities

The evidence from this study is that automotive models were readily transferred to China through U.S. foreign direct investment in China's automotive sector, but U.S. FDI did not substantially contribute to improving Chinese automotive-innovation capabilities because little knowledge about design and technology was transferred to China along with the products and manufacturing know-how. This study finds that there are five main reasons why U.S. FDI did not substantially contribute to improving Chinese innovation capabilities up to 2002 (see table 9.3):

• U.S. firms do not see themselves as responsible for "teaching" their partners how to improve basic capabilities.

Table 9.3
Explanations for why U.S. FDI has not substantially contributed to improving Chinese innovation capabilities

Explanation	Beijing Jeep	Shanghai GM	Chang'An Ford
U.S. firms do not feel responsible for "teaching" their partners.	✓	✓	✓
U.S. firms do not view their partners as sources of innovation.	✓	✓	✓
The structure of the joint ventures is inadequate.	✓	✓	✓
Chinese government programs and policies are weak or inconsistent.	✓	✓	✓
No binding international rules govern FDI.	✓	✓	✓

• U.S. firms basically view their counterparts in China as manufacturing partners, not as potential sources of innovation.

• The joint ventures were not structured to create the incentives for U.S. firms to transfer knowledge along with product.

• The Chinese government's inconsistent automobile industrial policies, weak R&D program, and lack of unambiguous performance standards resulted in weak Chinese firm-level capabilities.

• No binding international rules govern foreign direct investment.

Numerous Chinese business representatives and automotive experts interviewed in China bemoaned the continued laggardness of the Chinese automobile industry's innovation capabilities. According to the China Automotive Technology and Research Center (CATARC), "Before the reform and opening up to the outside world, the Chinese auto industry was 30 to 40 years behind that of the developed countries, whereas nowadays the level as a whole is 10 to 15 years . . . behind that of the advanced countries" (CATARC 2001, 15). One Chinese working for GM commented that foreign companies are not good teachers, but the Chinese companies are not good learners either (interview with GM

China Chinese employee A 2002). Another working for Beijing Jeep estimated that Chinese capabilities are at best "one-tenth" the level of U.S. capabilities (interview with a Beijing Jeep Chinese employee 2002). And an employee at Chang'An said that China has just learned the manufacturing process (interview with a Chang'An employee, Chongqing, 2002).

Another finding is that none of the U.S. firms believe they currently have a responsibility to "teach" their partners how to innovate and improve their technological capabilities. The U.S. firms do, however, teach their partners many other skills, such as how to install and operate manufacturing equipment, how to work with parts-and-components suppliers to maintain the quality of their products, how to run the business profitably, how to train the workers on the assembly line, and, in some cases, how to adapt products for the local market. In the case of Shanghai GM, GM argues that it has also learned some business skills from SAIC, so learning has ostensibly occurred in both directions. Recalling the typology of technological capabilities described in chapter 4, U.S. firms have transferred sufficient knowledge to their Chinese counterparts to give them production capabilities, and perhaps some limited project-execution capabilities. None of the U.S. firms, however, has tried to cultivate innovation capabilities in their Chinese partners.[14] All felt that they had no near-term incentives or responsibilities to develop these capabilities in their Chinese partners. As Wei-Ming Soh of DaimlerChrysler commented, "We are here to make money, not to do training. If it is worth it, we can do some training while we make money" (interview with W.-M. Soh, Beijing, 2002). To Soh, there must be a direct financial rationale for training.

GM's point of view was somewhat different. By investing in applied research projects in Chinese universities and investing in PATAC, GM is clearly making an effort to cultivate better technological capabilities in China, particularly in the realms of production and project execution. Yet one cannot argue, based on the evidence through 2002, that GM was trying to boost innovation capabilities in SAIC. But in early 2005, GM added $254 million to its investment in PATAC (Xinhua Economic News Service 2005a).

The availability of low-cost, highly educated and skilled researchers in China is also alluring to Ford. If the Chinese market becomes sizable and if there is a significant cost advantage for Chinese researchers, it might become worthwhile to Ford to focus on cultivating an innovative research staff in China. Because Ford is locked into an equal-ownership structure, it recognizes that it has to invest in the technological capabilities of Chang'An in the long term to be competitive in the Chinese market. Until 2002, Ford had made relatively modest physical investments in improving those longer-term capabilities inside the joint ventures (other than providing training and know-how). Keith Davey, director of Business Strategy, Asia Pacific and Africa for Ford, said that the investment in Chang'An's technological capabilities is proceeding on a step-by-step basis, building successive capabilities as the scope and complexity of the products expand. In addition, Ford said it would continue to support more advanced research at Chinese universities and institutes through Ford China's R&D fund (telephone interview with K. Davey, director, Business Strategy, Asia Pacific and Africa, Ford Motor Company, Dearborn, MI, 2003).

All of the U.S.-China joint ventures were structured with the primary goals of launching foreign automotive models into production in China to maximize the near-term profits of the joint ventures. In other words, the joint ventures are not structured to spark innovation in new technologies for the future—they are structured to manufacture and sell passenger cars in the present market. Yet the Chinese firms always held out hope that they would somehow acquire innovative capabilities through the joint ventures. Beijing Auto motive Industry Holding Company wished that American Motors Corporation would help it design a new model for the Chinese military, but AMC never had any intention to design one and was under no obligation to do so in the contract. To some in China, this attitude demonstrates that the U.S. firms have a short-term profit motive for China because otherwise, the U.S. firms would be trying to invest in improving capabilities for the long term. As a Chinese engineer at another company said, if their U.S. partner were more open technologically, there would be mutual benefit (interview with a Chang'An employee, Chongqing, 2002). But the lack of initiative on the part of the

Chinese firms to invest more in their own capabilities indicates their primary interest is also in generating short-term profits.

In the case of Shanghai GM, the Chinese government and SAIC tried to ensure that there would be more technology transfer by (1) insisting that the transfer be measured and verified, and (2) establishing a new technical center to help train Chinese workers and develop Chinese technical capabilities. SAIC also chose the first product that GM was to transfer—the Buick Century/Regal—but was worried about how to verify that GM transferred all the technology it was supposed to send. So SAIC developed a classification scheme to characterize the technological quotient of each type of technology. Not surprisingly, measuring the technology transfer proved difficult (interview with P. Murtaugh, chair and CEO, China Group, General Motors China, Shanghai, 2002). From GM's point of view, it agreed to put US$25 million into the Pan Asia Technical Automotive Center (PATAC) because such a center was obviously part of the price of winning the manufacturing joint venture with SAIC, and also because GM thought it could potentially become a competitive advantage. GM probably would not have established PATAC if it had not been a requirement to gain approval for the joint venture, but once GM made the investment, it was determined to develop PATAC into a good China-focused vehicle-development center. GM does not believe that PATAC will ever devote substantial resources to research, but PATAC is expected to substantially contribute to vehicle development (interview with P. Murtaugh, Shanghai, 2002).

Chang'An asked for a technical center during its negotiations with Ford, but Ford felt no particular obligation to respond to this request (telephone interview with K. Davey, Dearborn, MI, 2003). Thus, Ford did not establish a separate technology center with Chang'An. To the extent that the U.S. Big Three lobbied for the removal of technology-transfer requirements during the PNTR negotiations, they were in fact bargaining indirectly against further technology transfer within their own joint ventures.

This book concludes that the Chinese government failed to design and implement an aggressive, consistent strategy for the acquisition of technological capabilities from foreigners in the automobile industry. Such a strategy has been shown to be the key to the Korean automobile industry's success (Amsden 1989; Lee and Lim 2001). With the 1994 Auto Industry Policy, an attempt was made by the Chinese government to articulate such a strategy, but the implementation of this law was haphazard, and then the government effectively reversed its policies through its concessions regarding the auto industry on entry to the WTO. One Chang'An employee recommended that Chinese government regulations needed to be more stable and constant over time because there had been too much change. Moreover, according to him, there was too much inconsistency between the local and national government policies and that without government support of R&D, China's automobile industry would just become a manufacturing base (interview with a Chang'An employee, Chongqing, 2002).

The blame for Chinese laggardness cannot be placed on the government alone. The big Chinese automobile firms themselves have thus far failed to discipline themselves to invest in becoming more innovative. China's leading passenger-car producer, SAIC, did not set up its own R&D center until 2002 despite revenues of 120 billion yuan that year, for example (AFX European Focus 2003). A SAIC spokesperson said at the time that the establishment of the Automotive Engineering Academy of SAIC signified the beginning of China's efforts to develop automotive technology independently (Xinhua 2002b).

Two upstart Chinese firms, Geely and Chery, emerged during the late 1990s and broke into the market without foreign affiliations (although SAIC initially had a stake in Chery). Both firms have been accused of copying existing models in the market and have been sued by foreign firms (China Daily 2004), but at least they demonstrated initiative and the ability to get models into production without a foreign joint venture. This is not to say that these firms have advanced technological capabilities either, because there is some evidence that they hired foreign consultants to do the design- and product-adaptation work (interview with Geely employees, Ningbo, 2003).

The weakness and inconsistency of Chinese policy helps explain the variation in the levels of technology transferred over time. The three Sino-U.S. joint ventures were formed in the context of three distinct and differing policy periods. Beijing Jeep was formed before there was a formal industrial policy for the automobile sector. Shanghai GM was formed in the wake of the 1994 Auto Industry Policy when the government had decided it needed to build up domestic technological capability in this sector. Finally, Chang'An Ford was established in April 2001, seven months after the U.S. Senate had ratified the Permanent Normal Trade Relations (PNTR) bill, which removed most requirements on technologies.

Although technology transfer through FDI does not appear to have substantially contributed to innovation in China's automobile industry itself, there is some evidence from this study that the investment generated positive backward linkages to Chinese parts suppliers.[15] Because foreign firms were required to use a certain percentage of Chinese-made parts before China entered the WTO, the foreigners were forced to work with Chinese suppliers to improve the quality of their products. When product quality of the parts suppliers improved, they were able to expand their businesses and start exporting their products. Thus, the U.S. firms appear to have helped the Chinese parts-and-components companies to develop not just product capabilities, but also project-execution capabilities.

10

Limits to Leapfrogging and How to Overcome Them: Implications for Policy, Theory, and Future Research

The evidence from this study indicates that there are numerous practical limits to technological "leapfrogging" to substantially cleaner and more energy-efficient cars through technology transfer, because of the absence of proper incentives for the transfer of such technologies. Once these constraints are identified, strategies for how to overcome the limits through policy measures can be devised. This chapter will explore the apparent limits to leapfrogging based on the evidence from the three case studies in this book, and offer some options for how these limits could be overcome through new government policies. Indeed, with properly structured incentives, international technology transfer could be an effective tool for the deployment of cleaner and more energy-efficient automotive technology in China.

There are three realms of policy where the nature and extent of technology transfer from the United States to China can be affected: Chinese policy, U.S. policy, and international policy. These realms overlap with each other because U.S. and Chinese policies can target domestic affairs, bilateral relations, and global governance. Presently, Chinese policy has the most short-term potential to affect technology transfer to China, but, in the longer term, U.S. and international policy could have an equally strong effect. If policy in each of the three realms was coordinated toward achieving the same goals, the effectiveness of technology transfer as a means of deploying cleaner technologies could be significantly enhanced. The United States and China are more likely to coordinate their policies when their interests are aligned. On the imperative to reduce oil consumption and minimize harm to the environment, the fundamental interests of the United States and China are the same. These mutual interests have not been fully explored, however, because short-term economic interests in both countries have thus far dominated policy decisions.

Goldemberg was one of the first analysts to write about the potential of leapfrogging as it pertains to energy and environmental issues. He wrote:

Developing countries have a fundamental choice: they can mimic the industrialized nations, and go through an economic development phase that is dirty, wasteful, and creates an enormous legacy of environmental pollution; or they can leapfrog over some of the steps originally followed by industrialized countries, and incorporate currently-available modern and efficient technologies into their development process. (Goldemberg 1998, 730)

This insight is tremendously attractive because it reasonably assumes that if the advanced, cleaner technologies exist, they can be transferred to, and deployed in, developing countries.

This research shows that China's ability to "leapfrog" to substantially cleaner automobiles, using a strategy of knowledge acquisition through technology transfer from foreign firms, can be quite constrained in the absence of explicit incentives for the transfer of such technologies.[1] In other words, transfer of cleaner technologies through foreign direct investment does not automatically occur. This conclusion does not mean that the Chinese should not *try* to leapfrog to cleaner automobiles. Indeed, a primary motivation for this study was to determine how foreign firms could help China deploy the cleaner technologies that they developed in recent years.

First, the term *leapfrogging* must be defined in the context of the automobile industry in China. There are two kinds of leapfrogging that are most relevant to this analysis: (1) leapfrogging by skipping over generations of technologies, and (2) not only skipping over generations, but also leaping further *ahead* to become the technological leader. An example of the first kind of leapfrogging is the widespread adoption of cellular phones in China because the Chinese essentially skipped over wire-based communications technology to a wireless network. An example of the second kind of leapfrogging is illustrated by the performance of the Korean steel industry, which not only leapfrogged up to, but also eventually surpassed, the former top producers of steel to become one of the technological leaders of this industry.

There are two other kinds of technical change that are not necessarily "leapfrogging" but could result in the deployment of substantially cleaner or more energy-efficient automotive technologies in developing countries: (1) encouraging the use of the cleaner technologies, even if they do not require skipping generations of technologies; and/or (2) prohibiting the use of dirtier or inefficient technologies. For example, if the Chinese government decided to only allow the sale and use of highly efficient, gasoline-fueled cars, and to prohibit the use of large, "gas-guzzling" vehicles such as most conventional sport-utility vehicles (SUVs) for passenger-car use, China would have a more energy-efficient fleet than the United States currently does. Another example of the adoption of cleaner technologies is the Brazilian program to promote ethanol-fueled vehicles and discourage the use of conventional gasoline-fueled automobiles.[2] In this case, the Brazilian government purchased a guaranteed amount of ethanol through the state-owned oil company PETRO-BRAS, provided economic incentives for industries to produce ethanol (such as offering low interest rates and US$20 billion in loans (nominal dollars) to reach current installed capacity), and, most importantly, set the price of gasoline much higher than the price of ethanol to create a strong disincentive for the consumption of gasoline (Moriera and Goldemberg 1999). This program resulted in the avoidance of 9.45 million tons of carbon per year, corresponding to 18 percent of all carbon emissions in Brazil (Goldemberg 1998).[3]

Thus, technological change through adoption of incrementally cleaner and more efficient technologies may be sufficient to achieve the goal of cleaner-vehicle deployment without radical technological leapfrogging—especially as an interim strategy. Just as the combined effect of many incremental innovations is extremely important in the growth of economic productivity (Freeman 1992), incremental technological improvements can also be a major source of gains in environmental quality.

In the clean-vehicle context, what kind of technological change is leapfrogging? The answer to this question depends on the technology. Some, including China's Ministry of Science and Technology (MOST), believe that the advanced technologies that China should consider adopting are hybrid-electric or fuel-cell vehicles (Christenson 1997; Conte, Iacobazzi, et al. 2001; Burns, McCormick, and Borroni-Bird 2002). Do hybrid-electric and fuel-cell vehicles represent incremental or radical technological changes? Would they require leapfrogging? Commercially available hybrid-electric vehicles contain both a conventional gasoline engine and a battery-driven electric motor, and the two are used interchangeably when the automobile is in operation. At times, the gasoline engine is used, and at times the electric motor is used. The fuel savings are mostly derived from utilizing electric motors in stop-and-go urban driving, capturing wasted energy from braking, converting it into electricity, and storing it for later use by the electric-drive motor in a battery. Hybrid-electric vehicles vary in the degree to which they actually utilize the electric motor, but all hybrids take advantage of the main innovation—the *combined* use of electric and gasoline motors together to power the automobile (even though both kinds of motors have been in use separately for decades). So hybrid-electric automobiles are based, at least in part, on accumulated and incremental technological development, but the integration of the vehicle system is a radical innovation. Therefore, hybrid-electric vehicles can be considered a leapfrog-type innovation for passenger cars.

Fuel-cell vehicles (FCVs) are still in the R&D stage, and are not available commercially yet for passenger cars. FCVs also use an electric motor, but they abandon the gasoline-fueled engine entirely. Instead, fuel-cell vehicles use hydrogen as a fuel, and the hydrogen passes through a fuel cell to produce electricity, which runs an electric-drive motor. Again, FCVs can be considered, in part, the result of evolutionary or incremental technological change because many key components, such as electric motors and the fuel cells themselves, are not new inventions. Like the hybrid-electric vehicle, the fuel-cell vehicle could be considered a radical leapfrog-type innovation, however, because the electric motor and fuel cell are combined as a system for the first time for use in automobiles. Depending on how the hydrogen is generated, fuel-cell vehicles might require changes to the broader energy and transportation systems in China because new hydrogen generation and distribution networks might be required. It is also conceivable that the clustering of these technological changes could bring about a new technoeconomic paradigm if innovations in the energy-supply sector profound affected the entire economy, similar to how the discovery of cheap and plentiful oil enabled the mass production of automobiles and many other products. In the Chinese context, it is not clear that leapfrogging to fuel-cell vehicles would result in the environmental gains that are desired because hydrogen fuel would likely be made from coal due to the relative abundance of coal as a natural resource in China. If the carbon dioxide that resulted from the production of hydrogen were not captured and stored (thereby preventing the release of CO_2 to the atmosphere), a shift to hydrogen fuels for transportation in China based on coal-derived hydrogen could greatly increase greenhouse-gas emissions.

Limits to Leapfrogging

This book evaluates the efficacy of past technology transfer from U.S. to Chinese firms in the automobile industry. The question that remains is which lessons from this analysis can be applied to possible future leapfrogging in the Chinese automobile industry? Although all of the automobiles transferred from the United States to China from 1984 to 2002 contained conventional internal-combustion gasoline engines, the resulting modernization effect can be considered a leapfrog-type change for China in the sense of skipping generations, but not in terms of great gains in environmental quality. Between 1960, the year of the Sino-Soviet split, and China's reopening to the world during the late 1970s, automotive technology did not evolve at all within China. In the United States, however, automotive technology evolved significantly, especially due to the introduction of front-wheel drive and the computerization of many control technologies. Therefore, the foreign auto technology transferred to China beginning in 1983 effectively allowed China to skip over about twenty years of automotive technological development to a new generation of automobile technologies. These technologies were not substantially cleaner, however, because of the absence of Chinese pollution-control and fuel-efficiency regulations at the time.

Based on the past evidence, one might be tempted to conclude that it will be difficult for China to leapfrog to cleaner technologies such as hybrid-electric or fuel-cell vehicles for a number of reasons.[4] The costs of such automobiles (especially fuel-cell vehicles) are still higher than for conventional automobiles, and they would initially be harder to sell profitably until large economies of scale have been reached.[5] On the other hand, because China is a large potential market that is already growing rapidly, economies of scale might reached quickly. As output of such vehicles expanded, learning would certainly occur, and so unit costs would likely rapidly decline.

Also, based on the evidence from these cases, foreign firms will be reluctant to transfer technology that they consider to be at the cutting edge because of concerns about intellectual property rights. Foreign investment in such technologies has been substantial, and financial bottom-line concerns will always influence corporate decisions to transfer technologies. This study showed that intellectual property rights have not been a big concern for most of the U.S. firms in China so far, but U.S. firms have not yet been compelled to transfer really advanced technologies either. Chinese technological capabilities are still far enough behind, moreover, that they do not currently threaten foreign firms.

If technological capabilities for innovation are acquired gradually through learning by doing, then greater investments need to be made in China to improve the basic capabilities in production, adaptation, engineering, parts and components, and project execution, so that knowledge can be acquired for how to shift to advanced-technology automobile production. If China tries to skip to the world's technological frontier without assimilating enough knowledge about the conventional technologies on which many of the advanced technologies are based, China may fail to effectively leapfrog to clean technologies. As one study notes,

In establishing new production units, there is a tendency in developing countries to go for the latest technology—presumably to get on an equal footing with developed countries. . . . There is a danger, too, that selecting technology on or very near the frontier (without understanding how or why it works) can lock firms into a situation of continuously receding from that frontier as it advances. (Dahlman, Ross-Larson, and Westphal 1987, 764)

Foreign firms need to have compelling incentives to transfer any technologies not demanded by the market. In other words, the Chinese government would have to create a comprehensive system of incentives and penalties to elicit clean automobile technology transfer, and the government has not done so yet. The Chinese government has been inconsistent in its policy for the sector, requirements for technology transfer, and the development of related technological capabilities within Chinese firms. It has also lagged behind industrialized countries in terms of issuing and enforcing environmental performance standards. Similarly, the foreign firms have also failed to transfer vehicle technologies that are as clean as they are in the United States and Europe.

When considering whether China could skip to these advanced technologies without technology transfer from abroad, a number of different challenges come to mind. By many accounts, Chinese automotive technological capabilities still lag far behind the world level, so it is hard to imagine China being able to *catch up* in conventional technologies soon, much less imagine it *leapfrogging* to these more advanced clean automotive technologies without foreign technology transfer.

Another problem is that government, academic, and firm-based R&D programs for vehicles in China are still very small and not well connected to each other, so the general development of technological capabilities in China continues to be slow. Finally, the nature of the technological capabilities that would be required could be a real challenge for Chinese engineers because both hybrid-electric and fuel-cell vehicles require the capacity to integrate all the systems within an automobile, and this is perhaps the hardest type of capability to acquire (Chan 2002; interview with R. Frosch, Cambridge, MA, 2003).

The question of whether China can become the technological leader in these advanced automotive technologies is even more problematic, and it cannot be readily answered based on the findings of this study. There is no evidence so far that U.S. firms will teach their Chinese counterparts how to design, develop, and manufacture advanced, clean automobiles, but they might be willing to bring them into production with good intellectual property rights protections and no technology-transfer requirements. One emerging example is Toyota's announcement in 2005 that it would assemble the hybrid-electric Prius in China, but not actually transfer the knowledge about the technology to its partner, First Auto Works.

The current high reliance on foreign direct investment in the Chinese auto industry may continue to reduce China's incentive to innovate domestically. So long as Chinese firms can acquire reasonably modern products through its joint ventures with foreign firms, they have shown that they do not invest very much in improving their own capabilities.

There are also market-related problems influencing leapfrogging that China would have to overcome. First, because the market is not likely to produce the incentive to leapfrog to cleaner vehicles, the Chinese government would have to intervene. In contrast, in the case of mobile phones in China, the cost and market incentives were all strong. There was substantial consumer demand, the technology was coveted by the Chinese government, the survival of existing players was not threatened, and the revenues of existing Chinese firms were actually enhanced by leapfrogging to mobile phones (de Meyer 2001).

If China decides to leapfrog to hydrogen-fueled, fuel-cell vehicles, there is a problem with infrastructure. In the case of China's adoption of cellular phones, the fact that China could avoid installing a costly wire-based infrastructure was a huge incentive for leapfrogging to a wireless network. The opposite would be true for fuel-cell vehicles in China because an entire hydrogen infrastructure would have to be built.

Surmounting the Challenges and Pursuing a Strategy of Leapfrogging

There is no single best practice that the Chinese government and firms could employ to enable China to leapfrog to the technological frontier of clean automobiles; a combination of government policies, regulations, and nongovernmental initiatives is required. The main lesson from this study is that it would take a coherent, concerted, consistent, and long-term effort of government, industry, and civil-society cooperation to achieve such a goal. China's failure to "catch up" with the world level in conventional automotive technological capabilities is not a result of some inherent inability to do so. When China tries hard to become a world leader in a given sector, it has shown that it is capable of achieving that goal. Consider that China launched a manned rocket into space in 2003 and that it has developed its own domestic nuclear power designs. China's failure to develop the capabilities to design and produce world-class automobiles, much less leapfrog to hybrid-electric cars, can only be attributed to a lack of will.

In the short to medium term, a case might be made that China should concentrate on providing conventional but good alternative transportation options such as rapid bus transit while working to leapfrog to the most efficient, cost-effective, low-polluting commercially viable automotive technologies available (such as hybrid-electric vehicles). As the oil scenarios presented earlier show, in a best-case scenario, total vehicular Chinese oil consumption could readily be contained to less than 1 million barrels per day of oil consumption in 2020 through such measures, with related environmental and fuel-efficiency benefits. There is no reason that China needs to follow the practice of the United States with respect to fuel efficiency, which is essentially to delay the adoption of even more stringent fuel-efficiency standards in the hope that a big technological breakthrough will eventually provide a magical solution. Although initial fuel-efficiency standards in the United States were passed, these Corporate Average Fuel Economy standards have not been tightened since 1980, but billions of dollars have been spent on public-private partnerships like the Partnership for a New Generation of Vehicles and the current FreedomCAR program, with no widespread deployment of more efficient automobiles.[6] Meanwhile, the U.S. automobile manufacturers' association claims that the fuel efficiency of automobiles has improved, on average, about 2 percent each year. Automakers have not used those fuel savings to improve fuel efficiency. Instead, they have used the savings to increase vehicle weight, power, and the number of accessories. In contrast, the U.S. government constantly required automakers to reduce tailpipe emissions, and as a result, automobiles currently sold on the U.S. market emit remarkably few criteria air pollutants.

If China decides to go for the full leapfrogging strategy, it must approach the task comprehensively. China would need to improve its education system generally, and specifically the education of its automotive engineers. It would have to send its most promising workers overseas to study, and devise a strategy for luring those experts back to China to work in the industry. The Chinese government would have to promulgate policies to help foster a market demand for cleaner automobiles, such as raising the price of gasoline and implementing performance standards for air pollution and fuel efficiency that are continuously made more stringent over time. The Chinese government would have to force its domestic manufacturers to "learn by doing" increasingly on their own, without relying so heavily on the foreign manufacturers. And China would probably have to start developing capabilities in clean-vehicle components, such as automobile-scale fuel cells, until the Chinese producers acquire good enough system integration capabilities to fully participate in the innovation process—from invention to deployment—extracting "first-mover" profits from their brilliant innovations. Specific policy recommendations are provided next.

Implications for Chinese Policy

Chinese government policies and regulations are the most direct incentive for cleaner and more energy-efficient technology transfer to China. This study showed that when the Chinese government passed the first tailpipe-emission standards for automobiles in China, the U.S. joint-venture partners immediately transferred the requisite pollution-control technologies to bring their products into compliance with Chinese regulations. Representatives from all three of the U.S. manufacturers said in interviews that if the Chinese government passed a more stringent environmental law, the joint venture would certainly find a way to comply. Current Chinese environmental laws are not providing sufficiently strong incentives to provoke the transfer of the most appropriate, cost-effective, and cleaner automotive technologies. Not only are more aggressive Chinese emission and fuel-efficiency standards needed to elicit cleaner technology transfer, but these standards must also be implemented consistently and enforced vigorously. The lack of a strong inspection and maintenance regime in China will permit noncompliance with automotive emission standards. Another reason performance standards need to be set, maintained, and scheduled into the future is that they provide a rationale for Chinese firms to bargain for cleaner technologies from their foreign partners.

The absence of any Chinese fuel-efficiency policies or standards before 2005 caused China's oil imports for motor-vehicle consumption to increase rapidly until 2005, when the first fuel-efficiency standards for automobiles were set. The standards set for 2005 and 2008, while good first steps, will not provoke the transfer of significantly more fuel-efficient technologies such as hybrid cars because the standards are not that stringent. Indeed, although the 2005 and 2008 standards are tighter than the 2005 U.S. corporate-average fuel-economy standards, they are not nearly as stringent as the 2005 fuel-economy standards in Japan and the European Union (An 2004). Aside from further tightening the fuel-economy standards, the Chinese government could spur more demand for fuel-efficient automobiles among consumers by using fiscal tools such as tax incentives or increasing the price of gasoline in China (perhaps through a carbon tax, which would have the added benefit of targeting greenhouse-gas emissions), another initiative that the U.S. government has failed to undertake thus far.[7] The Chinese government has approved the imposition of a fuel tax in principle, but it has never implemented this tax (People's Daily 2003). It is almost inconceivable that U.S. firms would flout such regulations because it would be so embarrassing for the U.S. companies to fail to meet Chinese laws. Such regulations would create clear incentives to transfer cleaner and more efficient automotive technologies to China.

Other performance standards besides fuel-efficiency standards that are still needed to provoke the transfer of substantially cleaner vehicle technologies include standards for lower-sulfur fuels so that emission-control equipment will work properly in passenger cars. The lack of cleaner fuel was cited by U.S. manufacturers as a key reason why they did not transfer more advanced pollution-control equipment to China. In 2005, the Chinese government set a schedule for future pollution-control regulations from automobiles, so the focus for pollution control must now shift to cleaner fuels, enforcement of all these standards, and improving enforcement, inspection, and maintenance programs.

A second method for creating incentives for cleaner technology transfer is through the Chinese government's education policies and government-sponsored R&D programs. It has been confirmed that comprehensive educational systems play major roles in the assimilation of industrial knowledge (Rosenberg and Frischtak 1985; Sharif 1989). Innovative, capable workers need to be fostered through the educational system generally, and then specialized workers need to be given the opportunity to learn by doing. The most promising automotive engineers need to be sent overseas for training, and then lured back to China to work in the industry. In the case of Korea, for example, it was the government's large investments in human resource development that facilitated Korea's ability to acquire technological capabilities rapidly (Kim and Dahlman 1992). As one analyst notes, "Without adequate human capital or investments in R&D, spillovers from FDI may simply be infeasible" (Saggi 2002, 229). Such public investments would not only strengthen Chinese capabilities, but would also increase the bargaining power of Chinese firms at the negotiating table with their foreign partners.

If Chinese automotive engineers are innovative and capable of automotive design, the need of the Chinese automobile firms for their foreign partners will slacken. The Chinese Ministry of Science and Technology (MOST) has demonstrated vision and determination to develop and deploy cleaner vehicles in China with its "863" high-tech research program on electric, hybrid-electric, and fuel-cell vehicles. Enhancing the resources of this program (and continually working to improve it) will only fortify Chinese capabilities for cleaner automotive production in the future. Along with government-sponsored R&D, the Chinese government could also create incentives for the Chinese firms to become less reliant on foreign technology, and more innovative in their own right.

So far, market competition is proving to be a "double-edged sword" for China in the automobile sector. In many respects, the Chinese government's decision to lower trade barriers and foster increased competition in the domestic market should be credited with helping to modernize the industry. As demand for better automobiles soared in the 1990s, certain foreign manufacturers such as General Motors began to introduce newer, more attractive models into China, and this provoked the other foreign manufacturers to do the same. None of the newer models, however, came with the best-available, advanced, pollution-control technology for the reasons discussed in this study. Purely domestic Chinese manufacturers have been severely challenged by this competition. Some, like Chery and Geely, have responded to the competitive challenge, and are beginning to produce automobiles that are competitive within the Chinese market (but are not yet export-quality). Other Chinese firms are failing, and when they fail, jobs are lost, with all the related social repercussions.

Aside from issuing better performance standards for emission control and fuel efficiency, the Chinese government should also reassess its industrial policy for the auto sector. Because of China's many concessions to gain entry to the WTO, it is now prohibited from using many of its former tools for industrial development. During the 1980s, the lack of a well-defined policy for the automotive sector caused continued Chinese reliance on foreign technology. Once the Chinese government articulated an industrial policy in 1994, much more progress was made in acquiring better technological capabilities. Now that China has become a member of the WTO, it must consider which policy tools remain at its disposal for the cultivation of knowledge-based assets that will contribute to the future development of the industry. Such assets—the skills necessary to create new products or processes (Amsden 2001)—are essential for the further development of China's automobile industry.

Implications for U.S. Policy

The U.S. government presently has little influence over investment by U.S. firms in other countries. Former President Bill Clinton proposed creating environment and labor standards for international trade and investment in 1994 (Barber 1994), but he failed to accomplish this goal during his term in office. There is little current effort to push for such rules. There are three other means through which the U.S. government could promote the transfer of cleaner and more efficient automotive technology from the United States to China. First, if U.S. clean-vehicle policies and programs provoke innovation and reductions in the costs of clean automotive technologies, they could be transferred to China. Second, the United States could pursue a more concerted strategy of bilateral energy and environmental cooperation with China. Third, the U.S. government could use its power in multilateral forums to support the creation of internationally recognized standards for the conduct of investment and trade-related activities, including establishing protections for human health, environment, and energy conservation. Each of these options will be further elaborated in turn.

China represents a huge potential source of demand for cleaner automotive technologies. Most of the future growth in demand for automobiles is expected to come from rapidly growing industrializing countries, such as China. If the Chinese government sets increasingly stringent standards for pollution control and fuel efficiency, the demand for cleaner automotive technologies in China will be high. If these advanced technologies are invented in the United States, U.S. firms are positioned to be the primary suppliers of cleaner technologies in the future. So far, Japanese automotive firms are significantly ahead of U.S. firms in the commercialization of HEV technologies, and Toyota announced plans to assemble hybrid cars in China in 2005. Thus, the U.S. automotive industry is not only falling behind its competitors in Japan in the innovation of fuel-efficient technologies, but it may lose out in the Chinese market in this respect too. On the other hand, U.S. firms are still at the forefront of innovation in emission-control technologies.[8] If U.S. firms invent and develop the best fuel-efficient and clean-vehicle technologies, they will be positioned to transfer the technologies to China—but this study has shown that they will not necessarily do so without the appropriate incentives. Further-reaching performance standards in the United States are needed to continue to propel innovation in advanced vehicle technologies, especially with respect to fuel efficiency.

Because China has become the world's second-largest economy in purchasing-power-parity terms, it is easy to forget that it is still a developing country, home to millions of impoverished people. The U.S. government persists in denying foreign aid to China because it is a Communist country. This policy fails to reflect important U.S. interests in China, such as poverty alleviation and environmental protection. The logic of this prohibition is also inconsistent with the extensive economic ties between the two countries. Firms in the United States trade heavily with Chinese firms, invest in China, and profit from business interests in China. As of 2001, China was the United States' fourth largest trading partner (ITA 2003b). U.S. consumers greatly benefit from the lower prices of Chinese products. In January 2001, the U.S. Trade and Development Agency (TDA) was reauthorized to work in China after an eleven-year prohibition. The United States Export-Import Bank also is allowed to work in China. In 1999, a memorandum of understanding was signed between the Ex-Im Bank, U.S. Department of Energy, China Development Bank, and China State Development Planning Commission to establish a program to encourage U.S. firms to speed the deployment of clean energy technologies in China. This program originally offered China US$50 million in credit for renewable-energy projects, and the financing was later expanded to US$100 million for both renewable-energy and energy-efficiency projects. This program has not been heavily utilized. If the TDA and Ex-Im can be authorized to work in China, foreign aid for the protection of human health and the environment should be allowed too.

As a practical matter, it is in the U.S. national interest to give monetary aid and technical assistance to China for energy- and environment-related causes for two reasons. This study showed in chapter 2 that it is entirely possible that within two decades, China could import as much oil for transportation consumption as the United States currently imports today. If that were the case, world oil prices would certainly rise in response to this large new source of demand, with likely harm to the U.S. economy. This study has also shown that Chinese passenger cars could also be a major source of greenhouse emissions from motor vehicles within two decades, just as U.S. passenger cars currently are today. There is an opportunity to help China avoid emitting large quantities of greenhouse gases by transferring cleaner, more efficient technologies to China, and this would be in the U.S. interest because global climate change is likely to adversely affect the United States in a number of ways (Watson 2001).[9] At the same time, the United States should also improve its own fuel efficiency and reduce its own greenhouse-gas emissions in the transportation sector because the United States is the largest oil consumer and producer of greenhouse gases in the world.

Aside from increasing foreign aid, the United States could also work more cooperatively with China on a bilateral basis to create the incentives for clean technology transfer. There is a decades-long history of U.S.-China energy cooperation, dating back to 1979 when Deng Xiaoping and Jimmy Carter signed the Agreement on Cooperation in Science and Technology. There are now thirty protocols to this agreement, many of which cover energy- and environment-related topics. Two of the most relevant protocols to this research are the *Protocol on*

Cooperation in the Field of Fossil Energy, and the *Protocol on Cooperation in the Fields of Energy Efficiency and Renewable Energy Development and Utilization*. The latter agreement has many annexes, one of which is devoted to electric and hybrid-electric vehicles. Very little progress has been made on the implementation of this annex, so this is an area ripe for greater attention. For example, the two governments could initiate and support scholarly exchanges, the collection and dissemination of clean-vehicle-related data, and the study of mechanisms to facilitate the deployment of cleaner automotive technologies in both countries. One good example is the work the U.S. Environmental Protection Agency is doing cooperatively with China's State Environmental Protection Administration to address mobile-source emissions. In November 2004, EPA and SEPA established a work plan for vehicle emission control and transportation issues that listed areas of future cooperation such as fuel quality, in-use emission control, and heavy-duty diesel retrofits (Chuan 2004).

In a different realm of bilateral relations, that of trade and investment policy, the U.S. government has both facilitated and inhibited technology transfer to China. It facilitated technology transfer by pushing the Chinese government to create the conditions to encourage foreign direct investment, such as better protections for intellectual property rights. On the other hand, the U.S. government insisted that China not place any performance requirements, such as technology transfer, on foreign investors during the PNTR negotiations.

Finally, the United States could use its power in multilateral settings to create incentives for cleaner-technology transfer. It could ratify the Kyoto Protocol on global climate change to demonstrate a commitment to multilateral solutions for global environmental problems. Even if the United States wants to amend the Kyoto Protocol, ratifying it would demonstrate real commitment to reducing greenhouse-gas emissions around the world, and provide a legitimate way to do so. Also, the United States would show its determination to be a leader in finding solutions to the problem of climate change.

The U.S. government could also help devise an international agreement on investment that sets minimum standards for environmental performance, fuel efficiency, and the protection of human health. In trade agreements, the United States could support provisions to allow developing countries to enact domestic laws to protect the environment and human health without fear of retribution from any country or foreign firm. In recent years, the U.S. government has typically not supported such provisions. For example, Chapter 11 of the North American Free Trade Agreement (NAFTA) was written to provide protections for foreign investors from expropriations, but this provision subsequently has been appropriated by industry to subvert environmental regulations. Some companies have filed lawsuits against NAFTA governments over the enactment of environmental laws, arguing that these laws are tantamount to expropriation because the costs of compliance are so high. Naturally, such lawsuits can have a chilling effect on the passage of new environmental laws. As of March 2001, ten cases had been brought by companies against new environmental and natural-resource management laws of the three NAFTA states (IISD and WWF 2001). There have yet to be any rulings on these cases, but the effect has been to chill introduction of new environmental requirements.

Implications for International Policy

The evidence from this study indicates that in the absence of any international rules, Chinese domestic policies will most strongly affect the nature and extent of international technology transfer through foreign direct investment. On the other hand, if international rules were established, they could accomplish the same goal of provoking technology transfer for cleaner vehicles if the rules harmonized performance standards globally.

Presently, few international rules or policies govern foreign direct investment. The Trade-Related Investment Measures (TRIMS) agreement of the WTO only governs investment as it pertains to nondiscriminatory trade. For example, TRIMS prohibits local content requirements because they are viewed by the WTO as discriminating against products that do not contain local products. The one significant and historic attempt to create an international accord on investment was the OECD effort to devise a Multilateral Agreement on Investment (MAI). Because the draft MAI was perceived to be tilted so strongly to serve the interests of the investors (not the recipients of the investment), it was widely criticized and eventually abandoned. The OECD has since created the more sensitive Voluntary Guidelines for Multinational Enterprises that better take into account the interests of the recipient country, but these guidelines are not binding. In September 2003 in Cancun, the WTO was scheduled to begin discussing whether to launch negotiations within the institution of the WTO regarding foreign investment. But a coalition led by China, India, South Africa, and Brazil rejected the proposal to address rules for foreign direct investment under the auspices of the WTO at that meeting. Prior to 2003, WTO members limited themselves to organizing a working group in 1996 to study the relationship between trade and investment. Any new trade and investment agreements would need to allow developing countries, including China, to have some degree of latitude to create incentives for technology transfer. As one noted development economist argues, "Poor countries need the space to follow developmental policies that richer countries no longer require" (Rodrik 2001, 29).[10]

Weaker environmental standards theoretically can give a country a comparative advantage if the costs of compliance to meet the standards are high. There is no evidence, however, that U.S. or other foreign firms decided to invest in China's automobile industry because of China's relatively weaker environmental standards. Even so, U.S. firms have not transferred pollution-control technology to China that is nearly as clean as the technology they install in cars sold in the United States. The Chinese government has not imposed special rules on the foreign-invested joint ventures, even though those firms could easily transfer cleaner automotive technologies to their counterparts in China. If foreign investors were subject to international rules about environmental performance, they might be more inclined to transfer cleaner automotive technology to China.

A number of analysts have supported the notion of establishing minimum standards for foreign investment for environmental performance (French 1998; Zarsky 1999a). According to Zarsky, such rules would cover both microlevel investor responsibilities, and also macrolevel sustainability objectives. The establishment of minimum standards for environmental performance is an attractive idea because it would provide clear environmental rules for all investors, eliminate the potential comparative advantage that would derive from having lower standards, and reduce the potential for pollution havens in developing countries. Of course, individual countries should be allowed to set tighter standards if they wish to suit their particular needs and circumstances. Subsequent to the creation of minimum standards, however, countries might relax their own more stringent standards to the minimum level required internationally, which might cause an increase in pollution. Another concern is that individual countries might get "trapped in the mainstream," unable or unwilling to go beyond the international standard for political or economic reasons, even if there was a local need for more stringent standards. Some of the environmental challenges facing the world today require bold and courageous policy solutions, which minimum performance standards might not achieve. Yet, if standards were designed to achieve a social (i.e., environmental or human health) goal, and they were regularly reviewed and revised upward, they could be effective and consistent with WTO rules. For example, if a performance standard for carbon dioxide was set, but emissions of carbon dioxide from motor vehicles continued to rise unabated, the standard might have to be tightened. The European Union has devised a set of pollution standards that roll forward as the most polluting sources are dropped, and the average performance continually improves. Zarsky argues that such rules should govern all investment, not just foreign investment, so that there is no discrimination against foreign investment.

If they are negotiated in the future, global rules for trade and investment should be formulated on a multilateral basis in an open, inclusive, consensus-based process. International rules will only work if there is widespread support for them. Otherwise, countries will just flout the rules without fear of retribution.

Clearly, it is hard to measure and understand the effects of foreign direct investment on environmental quality without good information or data. In China, for example, no systematic and publicly available data on the fuel efficiency of automobiles were collected prior to 2005, the emissions of different pollutants from in-use automobiles remain unknown, and the amount of air pollution attributable to motor vehicles is still debatable. Thus, it is very difficult to measure the environmental effects of foreign direct investment in the auto sector in China. International institutions can help to standardize and collect this valuable information. Related to the need for better data collection and dissemination, there is also a need for some basic corporate-accountability mechanisms for foreign investors (Zarsky 1999a). There is ample evidence that if local communities have access to information about the companies operating in their cities and towns, they can make better-informed decisions about whether the firm is causing problems that need to be remedied.

Of course, another way to affect business practices internationally is through multilateral environmental agreements. The most relevant one for this research is the Kyoto Protocol, as previously mentioned. As of 2005, China had already signed and ratified the Kyoto Protocol, but the United States had not. If the United States joins this regime, there are a number of mechanisms in the protocol to help both countries reduce their greenhouse-gas emissions individually and cooperatively, such as the Clean Development Mechanism, Joint Implementation program, emissions trading, and common but coordinated policies and measures. An international carbon tax might be the most simple and economically efficient method to reduce greenhouse gases (Schmidheiny 1992), although there are potential impediments to this policy.

Implications for Theory

As discussed at length in chapters 8 and 9, the findings of this study have several implications for theory. These implications are summarized here:

1. There is little evidence in the case of U.S. technology transfer to the Chinese automobile industry for many of the leading hypotheses about the relationships between environmental policy, international trade, and foreign direct investment (including the pollution-haven, pollution-halo, race-to-the-bottom, and stuck-in-the-mud hypotheses).

2. There appear to be some practical "limits to leapfrogging" to substantially cleaner vehicle technologies through technology transfer from foreign firms in joint-venture arrangements. These barriers can be overcome through international investment rules, U.S. and Chinese policy, and the goodwill of foreign firms, but probably most effectively by Chinese regulations.

3. If technology is defined to include knowledge, foreign direct investment is not automatically an effective mechanism for technology transfer. Although many discrete technologies were transferred, Chinese firms acquired little "how-to" tacit knowledge from their U.S. joint-venture partners. If Chinese firms are not acquiring more advanced technological capabilities through their partnerships with foreign firms, they are not accumulating knowledge-based assets, which are considered fundamental for strong economic development.

4. Foreign direct investment is also not automatically an effective mechanism for transferring cleaner technologies to developing countries. Proponents of FDI argue that along with the actual investment, FDI brings modern technologies as well as cleaner products and practices. The evidence in the case of the Chinese auto industry is that U.S. FDI did not bring substantially cleaner automotive technologies to China until they were required by Chinese pollution-control regulations. As of 2005, none of the U.S. firms had transferred pollution-control technology to China comparable to what they produce and use in the United States.

5. Although U.S. firms transferred slightly cleaner technologies to China, the huge growth in the number of automobiles on the road vastly outweighs the potential technological benefit of these cleaner technologies. This means that the "scale" effect of producing so many more cars outweighs the "technique" effect of transferring slightly cleaner technologies.

6. The role of the state in technology transfer for industrial development appears to be very important. Chinese policy (or at times, the lack thereof) strongly affected the nature and extent of the technology transferred to China from U.S. firms.

7. The most important incentives for cleaner automotive technology transfer in these cases were market competition and Chinese government regulations. The most inhibitory barriers to cleaner automotive technology transfer were the lack of Chinese pollution-control and fuel-efficiency regulations, poor fuel quality, weak bargaining from Chinese firms, a vicious circle related to domestic competitiveness (or a marriage of convenience between the Chinese government and foreign auto companies), and a politically powerless environmental movement.

Implications for Future Research

This book provides the first study of firm-level technology transfer from the United States to China in the automobile industry from 1984 to 2002. Aside from updating this study in future years, there are two obvious comparative studies that would complement this research. First, it would be interesting to compare U.S. automotive technology transfer to China with U.S. automotive technology transfer to other developing countries with relatively large automobile markets, such as India, Mexico, and Brazil. This comparative analysis would allow the barriers and incentives to cleaner automobile technology transfer that were identified by this study to be tested in other developing-country contexts. Alternatively, U.S. automotive technology transfer to China could be compared with Japanese and European automotive technology transfer to China to test whether other foreign firms have transferred cleaner technologies to China than the U.S. firms have, and why (or why not).

Although not a big focus in this book, the apparent success of the Chinese automotive parts-and-components industry is intriguing because these Chinese supplier firms appear to have acquired more advanced capabilities than total-vehicle manufacturers in China. Why have the parts-and-components firms become more innovative than the big auto firms? My hypothesis is that Chinese government's local-content policies caused foreign firms to work with Chinese suppliers to bring their products up to specification, and so the foreign firms were forced to teach these suppliers.

Another tantalizing question that arose during this research was why U.S. firms were more interested in funding R&D activities at the Chinese universities rather than within their own joint ventures in China. Are the universities more innovative than firms in China? Does this practice indicate that U.S. firms trust university researchers more than they trust their manufacturing partners? What are the connections between Chinese universities and firms for technological innovation, and how could they be improved?

Finally, this book provides a preliminary analysis of the barriers and incentives for China to leapfrog to cleaner technologies, such as hybrid-electric or fuel-cell vehicles, using a strategy of acquiring these technologies from foreign firms through technology transfer. A more detailed and comprehensive analysis of this topic is warranted, especially to support the creation of policies that will facilitate this leapfrogging.

Conclusion

This study has documented that even though cleaner alternatives existed in the United States, relatively dirty automotive technologies were transferred to China during the 1980s and 1990s. In order for leapfrogging to significantly cleaner technologies in China to become a reality, either the foreign firms have to be compelled to transfer their cleaner technologies, or the Chinese firms have to develop their own capabilities for clean automobile development and production. There is little evidence that either alternative will happen soon, unless policies are formulated and implemented to shift gears and create the necessary incentives for the foreign and Chinese firms to change their past behavior.

Appendix A: Acronyms

AMC	American Motors Corporation
BAIC	Beijing Automotive Industry Holding Corporation
BJC	Beijing Jeep Corporation
CKD	Complete knockdown kit
CATARC	China Automotive Technology and Research Center
Chang'An	Chang'An Automobile (Group) Corp.
CNG	Compressed natural gas
CO_2	Carbon dioxide
DMC	Dongfeng Motor Corporation (Dongfeng)
EIA	U.S. Energy Information Administration, U.S. Department of Energy
EURO I–IV	European air pollution emission standards, phases I–IV
FAW	China First Auto Works Group Corporation
FCV	Fuel-cell vehicle
FDI	Foreign direct investment
GM	General Motors Corp.
HC	Hydrocarbons
HEV	Hybrid-electric vehicle
IPCC	Intergovernmental Panel on Climate Change
LPG	Liquefied petroleum gas
MAI	Multilateral Agreement on Investment
MFN	Most-Favored Nation (trading status)

MOFTEC	China Ministry of Foreign Trade and Economic Cooperation
MOST	China Ministry of Science and Technology
MPV	Multipurpose vehicle
NDRC	National Development Reform Commission
NOx	Nitrogen oxides
OBD	Onboard diagnostic system (for emissions)
OECD	Organization for Economic Cooperation and Development
OPEC	Organization of the Petroleum Exporting Countries
PATAC	Pan-Asia Technical Automotive Center
PNTR	Permanent Normal Trading Relations
R&D	Research and development
RMB	Renmenbi (Chinese currency)
SGM	Shanghai GM
SAIC	Shanghai Automotive Industry Corporation (Shanghai)
SAW	Second Auto Works (now DMC)
SDPC	China State Development Planning Commission
SEPA	China State Environmental Protection Administration
SETC	China State Economic and Trade Commission
SO$_2$	Sulfur dioxide
SUV	Sport utility vehicle (all-terrain)
SVW	Shanghai VW
TAIC	Tianjin Automotive Industrial (Group) Co. (Tianjin)
TRIMS	Trade-Related Investment Measures, WTO agreement
VW	Volkswagen
WTO	World Trade Organization

Appendix B: Chronology of Events

1913

• Model T Fords are exported to China.

1920s

• GM Buicks begin to be exported to China.
• Sun Yat-sen writes to Henry Ford, asking him to help build an automotive industry in China.
• Ford sets up a sales and service branch in Shanghai (1928).

1930s

• One out of every six automobiles on the road are Buicks.
• Japan invades China, beginning of Japanese-Chinese War (1937).

1947

• China becomes a founding member of the General Agreement on Tariffs and Trade (GATT).

1949

• People's Republic of China founded.

1949–1950

• Mao negotiates with Stalin for Sino-Soviet Treaty of Friendship, Alliance and Mutual Assistance.

1950

• First Taiwan Straits crisis.
• Nationalists in China withdraw from the GATT; Communists contest the withdrawal.
• Korean War begins.
• United States imposes trade embargo on China once Korean War starts.

1953

• China forms the first government oversight agency, the Automotive Industry Administrative Bureau, under the First Ministry of Machine Building.
• First Auto Works (FAW) established in Changchun.
• Soviets transfer ZIS 150 light-truck model to FAW, which became known as the *Jiefang* (liberation).

1958

• Great Leap Forward begins.
• Second Taiwan Straits crisis.
• FAW produces its first passenger car, the *Hongqi* (Red Flag) black sedan, based on Daimler-Benz's 200 model.
• Shanghai Automotive Assembly Plant (now Shanghai Automotive Industry Corporation—SAIC) produces its first passenger car.
• Chang'An Machine-Building Plant produces first all-terrain vehicle, using technology imported from the U.S.S.R.

1960

• Soviet Union withdraws all economic assistance.
• Major famine in China through 1961.

1963

· China produces a grand total of eleven cars.

1964

· Third Front campaign launched, spurring establishment of many rural automobile factories, most notably the Shiyan Number Two Automobile Factory (known as Second Auto Works), now called Dongfeng Motor Corporation.
· October 16, 1964, China explodes its first atom bomb.

1965

· China National Automotive Industrial Corporation (CNAIC) is formed to oversee auto companies and coordinate planning for the industry.

1966

· Cultural Revolution launched.
· Passenger-car production ceases.
· CNAIC is eliminated.

1969

· China opens back up to the world.
· U.S. National Security Advisor Henry Kissinger secretly flies to China to open up communication channels between the United States and China.

1971

· Premier Zhou Enlai invites U.S. national Ping-Pong team to Beijing to play against Chinese team.
· United Nations admits the People's Republic of China to its General Assembly after twenty-two years.

1972

• President Richard Nixon flies to China to meet Chairman Mao Zedong, and they write the Shanghai Communiqué.

1976

• Mao Zedong dies.
• Cultural Revolution officially ends.
• Downfall of Gang of Four.

1978

• Law on Joint Ventures is promulgated in China, creating the initial framework for foreign direct investment (FDI) in China.

1979

• Formal normalization of relations with the United States.
• President Jimmy Carter and Vice Premier Deng Xiaoping sign Agreement on Cooperation in Science and Technology.

1980

• China applies for observer status at the GATT.
• Chinese government imposes tight import restrictions on passenger cars.

1982

• China is granted observer status at the GATT.
• State Council reinstates the China National Automotive Industry Corporation (CNAIC).

1983

• Beijing Jeep joint venture established between American Motors Corporation (AMC) and Beijing Auto Works (BAW).

1984

- China officially permits the private ownership of cars.
- Shanghai VW joint venture established between Shanghai Automotive Industry Corporation and Volkswagen.
- Import restrictions are temporarily relaxed.

1986

- Licensing agreement between Tianjin Automobile Xiali Company (TAIC) and Daihatsu for acquisition of Xiali car model (used as taxis in Beijing and other northern cities).
- China applies for full membership at the GATT.
- State Council releases Provisions for the Encouragement of Foreign Investment (October 11).

1987

- CNAIC is designated an "association" and loses significant power.

1988

- Top Chinese political leaders announce "Big Three, Little Three" industrial plan to consolidate the dozens of auto companies into six major firms.

1989

- Tiananmen Square massacre (June).
- Formal normalization between Russia and China negotiated by Deng Xiaoping and Mikhail Gorbachev.
- Chinese government again imposes tight import restrictions.

1990

- FAW-VW joint venture between First Auto Works and Volkswagen established.
- Dongfeng Citroën joint venture between Dongfeng Motor Corporation (formerly Second Auto Works) and Citroën established.

• CNAIC is reinstated as a "corporation" but its governmental authority is unclear.

1991

• Eighth Five-Year Plan is published, designating the auto industry as a "pillar industry" (along with electronics, machine building, and petrochemicals).

1992

• Guangzhou Peugeot joint venture established between Guangzhou Automotive Manufacturing Corporation and Peugeot.
• Ford opens a representative office.
• Jinbei GM joint venture established between FAW Jinbei Automotive Company and General Motors to produce light trucks.
• Dongfeng Motor Corporation and the French company, Citroën, form US$800 million joint venture.

1993

• Chang'An Suzuki joint venture established between Chang'An Automobile (Group) Corp. and Suzuki Motor Corporation.
• China becomes a net oil importer.

1994

• New Automotive Industry Policy announced by State Planning Commission (February).
• GM China office opens in Beijing.

1995

• Negotiations for Shanghai GM joint venture begin.
• Ford establishes Ford Motor China Ltd.
• Jinbei GM closes down for four years.

1997

• Shanghai GM joint venture between Shanghai Automotive Industry Corporation and General Motors established. Separately, the Pan Asia Technical Automotive Center is established between the same two firms.
• Guangzhou Honda is established, with Honda taking over the ownership of the foreign share in the joint venture with Guangzhou Automotive Manufacturing Corporation, formerly held by Peugeot SA.

1998

• Dongfeng Yueda-Kia established between Dongfeng Motor Corporation, Jiangsu Yueda Group, and Kia Motor of Korea.

1999

• Regular production of Shanghai GM Buick New Century sedan begins (April).
• Negotiations on Permanent Normal Trade Relations (PNTR) status between the United States and China conclude (November).
• Jinbei GM reestablished.
• Jiangsu Nanya Auto Company—a joint venture between Yuejin Motor Corporation and Fiat Auto S.p.A—is established in Nanjing.
• China launches Clean Vehicle Action program to deploy alternative-fueled vehicles.
• China Ministry of Science and Technology (MOST) launches research program to develop electric vehicles in China and creates an electric demonstration project in City of Shantou.

2000

• General Motors donates five electric vehicles to MOST (September).
• U.S. Senate passes PNTR bill (September), paving the way for China to join the World Trade Organization. The PNTR agreement enters into force in October. PNTR specifies many changes for foreign direct investment in China and for policies governing the automotive sector in particular, including:
 · Phasing down tariffs on all vehicles to 25 percent by 2006
 · Phasing down tariffs on auto parts to 9.5 percent by 2006

· Eliminating quotas by 2005

· Opening the auto-financing market fully to foreign investors

· Eliminating any export performance, trade, foreign-exchange balancing, and prior-experience requirements as criteria for trading rights

· Eliminating conditions on investment, including performance requirements, local content, export performance, technology transfer, offsets, foreign-exchange balancing, or R&D

· Abiding by the Trade-Related Investment Measures (TRIMS) agreement of the WTO

· Eliminating all subsidies that are prohibited under WTO rules

• First Buick Sail is produced (December).

• Fengshen (Aeolus) Automotive Co. (also known as Guangzhou Nissan) is established as a joint venture between Dongfeng Motor Corporation, Jing'An Yunbao Motor Company, and Yulon Motor Company (a Taiwanese firm 25 percent owned by Nissan) to produce the Aeolus Bluebird.

• China requires that all new cars produced in China must have a catalytic converter and meet EURO I emission standards. New cars in Beijing, Shanghai, and Chongqing have to meet EURO II standards.

• Leaded fuel is banned.

2001

• Chang'An Ford joint venture is established between Chang'An Automotive Company and Ford Motor Company in Chongqing (April).

• Chevy Blazer begins production at Jinbei GM (May).

• Buick Sail (compact car) begins regular production at Shanghai GM (June).

• FAW and Mazda agree to start production at FAW Hainan Motor Company.

• China becomes the 143rd member of the World Trade Organization.

• China's Ministry of Science and Technology launches major R&D initiative in its "863" (High Tech) Program for the development and deployment of electric, hybrid-electric, and fuel-cell vehicles during the 10th Five-Year Plan (2001–2005) period.

• 10th Five-Year Plan for auto industry is released, setting the following goals for the industry by 2005:

· Total output of passenger cars shall reach 1.1 million.

· Added value of entire motor-vehicle industry (including trucks and motorcycles) shall reach US$15.72 billion (1 percent of GNP).

· Passenger cars will comprise 35 percent of total vehicle-fleet mix.

· Independent development capabilities will be strengthened.

· Carburetor cars will be banned as well as those using CFC-12 air conditioners.

· Energy-efficiency rules for vehicles will be formulated and stricter emission controls issued.

· State-level R&D centers at major automotive enterprises will be created that will receive preferential treatment.

· Further development of the auto parts-and-components industry will be encouraged.

2002

• First Auto Works takes over Tianjin Automotive Xiali Company and they sign a joint venture with Toyota.

• Dongfeng and Nissan sign a memorandum of understanding to form a new joint venture.

• SAIC-Wuling-GM announce a new joint venture to produce minibuses.

• Beijing Hyuandai joint venture established between Beijing Automotive Industry Holding Company and Hyundai Motor Company.

• SAIC invests in Daewoo with GM (the first example of foreign direct investment by a Chinese automobile company) (October).

• China produces a million passenger cars for the first time in one year.

• China permits two purely domestic firms to begin producing passenger cars—Geely Group in Zhejiang Province, and Brilliance Automotive in Shanghai.

2003

• Shanghai GM buys new factory in Yantai, Shandong Province, in order to double its capacity.

2004

• The Chinese government announces a set of proposed fuel-efficiency standards.

• The Chinese government issues a revision of its 1994 Auto Industry Policy.

2005

• China's first fuel-efficiency standards for automobiles take effect.

Appendix C: Major Sino-Foreign Joint Ventures in the Chinese Automobile Industry, 1984–2005

Chinese partner	Joint venture (location)	Foreign partner, dates	Total investment (US dollars) and ownership
Shanghai Automotive Industry Corp. (SAIC)	Shanghai Volkswagen (Shanghai)	Volkswagen (1984–present)	50% VW, 25% SAIC, 25% Bank of China and CNAIC
First Auto Works (FAW)	FAW-Volkswagen (Changchun, Jilin)	Volkswagen (1990–present)	$540 million, 40% VW, 60% FAW
Dongfeng Motor Corp. (formerly Second Auto Works)	Dongfeng Citroën (Wuhan, Hubei)	Citroën (1992–present)	$800 million, 30% Citroën, 70% Dongfeng
Tianjin Automobile Xiali Company (TAIC)	Tianjin Automobile Xiali Company (TAIC)—First Auto Works (FAW) (Tianjin)	Licensing agreement with Daihatsu (1986–1993), initial arrangement with Toyota in 2000 before FAW takeover in 2002 (see below)	
Shanghai Automotive Industry Corp. (SAIC)	Shanghai GM (Pudong, Shanghai)	General Motors Corp. (1997–present)	$1.2 billion with 50% SIAC, 50% GM
Guangzhou Automotive Group	Guangzhou Honda Automobile Co. Ltd. (Guangzhou, Guangdong)	Honda Motor Co. (1998–present)*	$141 million, 50% Guangzhou, 50% Honda
Chang'An Automobile (Group) Corp.	Changan Suzuki (Chongqing)	Suzuki Motor Corp. (1993–present)	51% Chang'An, 35% Suzuki, 14% Nissho Iwai (Japan)
Dongfeng Motor Corp. and Jing'An Yunbao Motor Co.	Fengshen (Aeolus) Automotive Co. Ltd. (also known as Guangzhou Nissan)	Yulon Motor Corp. (Taiwan, 25% owned by Nissan) (2000)	45% DMC, 25% Yulon (Taiwan), 30% Yunbao

Chinese Partner	Joint Venture	Foreign Partner	Ownership
Yuejin Motor (Group) Corporation	Jiangsu Nanya Auto Co., Ltd. (Nanjing, Jiangsu)	Fiat Auto S.p.A. (1999–present)	50% Fiat, 50% Yuejin
FAW Jinbei Automotive	Jinbei GM (Shenyang, Liaoning)	General Motors Corp. (1992–1995, 1999–present)	50% FAW Jinbei, 50% GM
First Auto Works Car Co.	FAW Hainan Motor Co.	Mazda (Ford owns 33.4% of Mazda) (2001–present)	17.5% Mazda, 82.5% FAW
Beijing Auto Works (BAW)	Beijing Jeep (Beijing)	DaimlerChrysler originally with AMC (1983–present)	42.4% DaimlerChrysler, 57.6% BAIC
Jiangsu Yueda Group (originally), later Dongfeng Motor Co.	Dongfeng Yueda-KIA (Jiangsu)	Kia Motor (1998–)	30% Jiangsu Yueda, 50% Kia, 20% Dongfeng (as of 2000)
Beijing Automotive Industry Holding Corporation (BAIHC)	Beijing Hyundai Motor Co.	Hyundai Motor Co. (2002–)	$400 million, 50% BAIHC, 50% Hyundai
First Auto Works (FAW) and Tianjin Auto Xiali Co.	FAW-Tianjin-Toyota (Changchun and Tianjin)	Toyota Motor Corp. (2002–)	$2.5 billion, 50% Toyota, 50% FAW
Chang'An Automobile (Group) Corp.	Changan Ford (Chongqing)	Ford Motor Co. (2001–present)	$98 million with 50% Chang'An, 50% Ford
Dongfeng Motor Co.	Dongfeng Nissan (Hubei)	Nissan (2002)	$2 billion, 50% Dongfeng, 50% Nissan

Notes

Chapter 2

1. Industry consumes a large portion of China's oil, and electricity generators a smaller fraction (LBNL 2001).

2. Note that it is estimated by CATARC that the average number of miles driven each year by private passenger cars is 18,640 (Wu, personal communication, Tianjin, 2003).

3. In rural areas, indoor air pollution caused by burning biomass and coal for heating and cooking is the biggest concern. Overall, motor vehicles are not the largest source of national air pollution, but they are the biggest source of concern in the cities.

4. Author's calculations as follows: X million bbls/day * 6 GJ/bbl * 20 kgC/1 GJ oil * 365 days/year * 1,000 metric tons/GgC = X million metric tons C. China's annual carbon emissions were estimated to be about 700 million metric tons in 2000.

Chapter 3

1. According to the World Bank (2005a), purchasing power parity (PPP) is a "form of exchange rate that takes into account the cost and affordability of common items in different countries." 2000, China's gross national income (GNI) was US$1.1 trillion and its PPP GNI was US$4.95 trillion. That same year, the U.S. GNI was US$9.6 trillion and its PPP GNI was also US$9.6 trillion.

2. The World Bank's 2000–2001 *World Development Report* on poverty estimated that in 1998, there were 60 million people below the poverty line in China (World Bank 2000).

3. The "Chinese auto industry" here includes the automobile, motorcycle, engine, and parts-and-components industries.

4. Most foreign investment goes to industrialized countries. In 2001, 65 percent of total foreign direct investment went to developed countries, not including Central and Eastern Europe (UNCTAD 2002).

5. Purely Chinese-made cars represents small fraction of passenger-vehicle production. At most, 19 percent of the total number of passenger vehicles produced are estimated to be made by firms without foreign affiliations (CATARC 2002a). All of the major Chinese passenger-car producers have formed joint ventures with foreign firms.

6. Total Chinese imports in 2002 were valued at US$295 billion, making oil imports account for about 5 percent of total imports (EIU DataServices 2003).

Chapter 4

1. See also Dahlman, Ross-Larson, and Westphal 1987.

2. Chang'An is but one of many automobile producers that sprang from the weapons industry. As of 1995, the government-owned China National Ordnance Industry Corporation (CNOIC) owned 120 automakers in China. The automotive divisions accounted for 60 percent of CNOIC's output value, and 90 percent of the profits of the whole weapons sector (FBIS 1995).

3. Amsden (2001, 140.) cites Mahn-Je Kim, president of the Korea Development Institute, who stated that "Korean automobiles faced severe market competition in the export frontiers. However, it was not market competition that stimulated the industry to grow strong enough to venture into the world market. I am not arguing that market competition was useless. Rather, I would like to point out that the *environment* was provided in which the private sector's creativity and responsibility could be maximized."

Chapter 5

1. Nash and Kelvinator, and Hudson and Studebaker, had recently merged into the two respective companies that then merged to become American Motors Corporation.

2. This joint venture never materialized.

3. In 2000, DaimlerChrysler had entered into a strategic "alliance" with Mitsubishi. DaimlerChrysler Group (as a whole) is Mitsubishi's largest shareholder, owning 37.3 percent of Mitsubishi's stock as of March 2002.

4. Mitsubishi Motors also owns 2.84 percent of Hyundai as of 2002.

Chapter 6

1. This includes cars produced in SAIC's joint ventures with SGM and SVW.

2. In 1996, the total number of passenger cars produced was 370,821. SVW produced 200,031, 54 percent of the total.

3. This luxury model is now called the Buick Regal in China.

4. Hu Maoyuan was the first president of Shanghai GM, but he was later promoted to the positions of president and CEO of SAIC overall.

5. SGM puts an 80,000-mile guarantee on their car's ability to meet the EURO II standard.

Chapter 8

1. These two agencies were combined into a new State Reform and Development Commission in early 2003.

2. The second proposition—that if trade liberalization produced economic growth and higher national income, the country would "naturally" respond by imposing more stringent pollution controls and enforcing environmental laws more vigorously—is credited as the first statement of what is now called the "environmental kuznets curve" hypothesis. The hypothesis is that there is an inverted U-shaped correlation between per capita income and environmental quality. As per capita income increases, environmental quality worsens, but once income reaches a certain level, environmental quality begins to improve. This hypothesis will not be evaluated here with respect to air pollution in China. It is sufficient to note that Grossman and Kruger's controversial hypothesis has been the subject of much debate and criticism as reviewed by David Stern (2002).

3. The word *sustainable* is often used in the literature about environmental technology transfer. A "sustainable" process or condition is defined as "one that can be maintained indefinitely without progressive diminution of valued qualities inside or outside the system in which the process operates or the condition prevails" (Holdren, Daily, et al. 1995, 3). Thus, without radical sociotechnical breakthroughs, it is hard to imagine that any automotive technology transferred from the United States to China in the next few decades could ever be deemed "sustainable." It would be unsustainable because all internal combustion vehicles burn fossil fuels and produce air pollutants as byproducts. Automotive technologies such as the hybrid-electric engine exist, however, that could substantially reduce local air-pollution damage even if they could not eliminate it. In addition, such fuel-efficient technologies could reduce the rate of automotive emissions of greenhouse gases (especially carbon dioxide) into the atmosphere. Reducing the rate of greenhouse-gas emissions would give humans and ecosystems more time to adapt to climatic disruptions because the rate of climate change itself would also decelerate (Watson 2001). Holdren, Daily, and Ehrlich (1995) state that constraining the rates of degradation of monitorable environmental stocks to not more than 10 percent per century would be prudent practice. There are some automotive technologies on the horizon (such as fuel cells) that could theoretically drastically reduce pollution enough to actually contribute to "sustainable" automobile development if deployed widely. Until they are deployed, however, automobile technologies transferred to China that improve air quality can only be termed "cleaner," not "sustainable."

4. The IPCC does not seem to disagree. It advocates taking a country-by-country approach to identifying, analyzing, and prioritizing the particular barriers to technology transfer. They argue that it is "important to tailor action to the specific barriers, interests, and influences of different stakeholders in order to develop policy tools" (Metz, Davidson, et al., 2000, 19).

5. In their study, "Importing firms cited environmental regulation as the primary motivating consideration, and exporters said that demand was low in countries that lacked sufficient regulation to require such technology" (Lanjouw and Mody 1996, 566).

Chapter 9

1. It was not possible to evaluate Chang'An Ford's performance in this respect because this joint venture began production so recently.

2. The phrase "distributorless engines" refers to replacing mechanical, rotating high-voltage distribution mechanisms with static electronically controlled components for the ignition system. They can be used in conjunction with other electronic functions, such as electronic fuel-injection systems (Adler 1986).

3. The only Japanese automaker to invest in a joint venture in China until the late 1990s was Suzuki, which established a partnership with Chang'An in 1993, as discussed in chapter 7. Other Japanese companies were relatively late to the Chinese market in terms of direct investment. Honda took over Peugeot's failed joint venture in 1997 and began to produce Honda Accords at that factory in Guangzhou. Toyota invested in a new joint venture with Tianjin Automobile Xiali Company (TAIC) and First Auto Works (FAW) in 2002. During the early 1980s, Daihatsu licensed relatively old compact-sedan technology to TAIC; this technology is still in production in Tianjin.

4. Joseph A. Schumpeter distinguished three important phases in tech development: invention, innovation, and diffusion. Invention is the first demonstration of a new solution. Innovation is when a newly discovered material or technique is put into regular production. Diffusion is the widespread replication of the technology and its assimilation in a socioeconomic setting (as described by Grubler 1998, 24).

5. Kenneth Arrow (1969, 31) was one of the first to note that one could learn by doing because "the motivation for engaging in the activity is the physical output, but there is an additional gain, which may be relatively small, in information which reduces the cost of further production."

6. Eli Heckscher wrote "The Effect of Foreign Trade on the Distribution of Income" in 1919, then Bertil Ohlin elaborated on Heckscher's theory of trade in his book *Interregional and International Trade* in 1933. The two publications together provide the Heckscher-Ohlin theory. This theory of comparative advantage as the basis for international trade made the simplifying assumption that different nations use the same technology. According to one analysis, "The

assumption that both nations use the same technology means that both nations have access to and use the same general production techniques" (Salvatore 1993, 108).

7. To Schumpeter, the concept of "new combinations" in economic development includes the (1) introduction of a new good—or of a new quality of a good; (2) introduction of a new method of production; (3) opening of a new market; (4) "conquest" of a new source of supply of raw materials or half-manufactured goods; and (5) carrying out of the new organization of any industry, like the creation of a monopoly position or the breaking up of a monopoly position (see Schumpeter 1934, 66). In discussing Schumpeter's other major contributions to the theory of technological change, Grubler (1998) notes that Schumpeter had the two important insights that technologies are evolved from *within* (that technological change should not be exogenous to economic-growth models), and that technological change is inherently dynamic and not static.

8. For example, in 1969 Kenneth Arrow wrote, "A production function is defined relative to a given body of technological knowledge" (p. 29).

9. Author's emphasis.

10. Saggi (2002) notes in the *World Bank Research Observer* that there are three potential channels of spillovers: demonstration effects (where firms adopt technologies through imitation or reverse engineering), labor migration (workers move to other firms and carry their knowledge with them), and vertical linkages (otherwise known as backward and forward linkages). The idea of vertical linkages rests on the concept that a foreign investment in one industry can indirectly produce benefits in other related industries. For example, suppliers of automotive parts and components may benefit from having a new source of demand for their product if there is FDI into a manufacturer. This would be an example of a "backward" linkage.

11. The Trade-Related Investment Measures (TRIMS) agreement under the WTO applies only to investment measures related to trade in goods, but not services. Moreover, according to the WTO, "TRIMS is not concerned with the regulation of foreign investment" (WTO 2003b). The TRIMS agreement does prohibit local-content requirements because they are seen as discriminating between imported and domestic products.

12. These guidelines were originally established as part of the OECD Declaration on International Investment and Multinational Enterprises, adopted by the OECD governments in 1976 to facilitate direct investment among OECD members.

13. Including Hong Kong (which received US$22 billion alone in 2001), China received US$69.6 billion in 2001, more than twice as much as Mexico, which ranks second as a developing-country recipient of FDI at US$24.7 billion in 2001 (UNCTAD 2002). However, China does not receive as much foreign direct investment as some of the most industrialized nations.

14. As discussed in the introduction to chapter 4, production capabilities include management of established facilities, production engineering, repair and

maintenance of physical capital, troubleshooting, and adaptation of products and processes as needed. Project-execution capabilities include personnel training, preproject feasibility studies, project management, project engineering, procurement, plant construction, and start-up of operations. Innovation capabilities include the skills necessary to create new processes and products (ranging from basic science to product development). See Dahlman, Ross-Larson, and Westphal 1987; Amsden 2001.

15. See the discussion of backward linkages in chapter 3.

Chapter 10

1. Limits to leapfrogging to cleaner energy technologies have also been identified in East Africa, where the social conditions and economic realities of rural life limit the capacities of rural households to absorb new technologies (Murphy 2001).

2. Moriera and Goldemberg 1999. Also, it should be noted that Goldemberg considers the ethanol example to be one of leapfrogging.

3. I did not attempt to study whether alcohol derived from sugarcane would be an effective strategy for China.

4. The Ministry of Science and Technology in China is trying to demonstrate the feasibility of battery electric vehicles in its electric-vehicle demonstration project in Shantou, Guangdong Province. The advantage to electric vehicles is that China could avoid importing large quantities of oil for use in motor vehicles if it could power vehicles with coal-generated electricity.

5. But niche markets could be exploited.

6. By the time PNGV was canceled, the U.S. government had spent approximately US$1.25 billion, or US$250 million per year on average according to the U.S. General Accounting Office. DOE had provided half of the funding, NSF and the Department of Commerce together provided about 40 percent, and EPA and the Department of Transportation also funded about 10 percent. However, 45 percent of this funding reportedly was only indirectly relevant to its goals or was not coordinated through PNGV (GAO 2000, 52). Officials at DOE estimate that even though the need was approximately US$600 million per year, the peak annual allocation was only US$166 million, not including NSF money (interview with E. Wall and P. G. Yoshida, U.S. Department of Energy employees, Washington, D.C., 2002). Although only one estimate of industry spending has been made, it appears that industry could have spent much more than the federal government—and a far greater share of total investment than the program had envisioned. In the National Research Council's sixth peer review of PNGV, they estimated that for FY1999 alone, the three companies together spent US$980 million. Estimates of investments for each of the previous years were comparable (NRC 2000, 114). However, no detailed accounting of how this money was spent is provided in the NRC report, making it difficult to assess how much of

the US$980 million was directly spent on PNGV research or whether some of this spending went to indirectly related projects.

7. Revenues from such a tax could be used to enforce the environment and health-related standards and regulations, for additional R&D on cleaner technologies, and for developing additional technological capacity for clean-vehicle deployment.

8. Innovation in cleaner technologies for all major multinational automobile firms was initially sparked by California's strict regulations on pollution control and fuel efficiency (Van Vorst and George 1997). The U.S. federal government tends to lag behind California in terms of vehicular pollution-control legislation, but once a regulation has proved feasible in California, the U.S. government often adopts the California rule.

9. Once carbon dioxide is emitted, it has a half life in the atmosphere of the order of one hundred years, so releases of greenhouse gases cannot be readily reversed. Carbon dioxide can be absorbed in plants and oceans; this process is known as carbon sequestration. According to the Intergovernmental Panel on Climate Change, it is not clear how much carbon can be absorbed by these sources (Watson 2001). Therefore, it is preferable to prevent emissions of greenhouse gases wherever possible.

10. Rodrik (2001) does not endorse any specific policies, such as policies to provoke technology transfer, at this point in his article. He simply writes, "For example, poor countries might be allowed to subsidize industrial activities (and indirectly their exports) when this is part of a broadly supported development strategy aimed at stimulating technological capabilities" (p. 38).

References

Adler, U., ed. 1986. *Automotive Handbook*. Stuttgart: Robert Bosch GmbH.

AFX-Asia. 2005, May 25. "China's Changan Auto, Ford, Mazda Get Green Light for Engine JV." *AFX News Limited*. Beijing.

AFX European Focus. 2003. "SAIC 2002 Sales Double to 610,000 Units; Revenue Up 22.4 pct to 120 bln yuan." *AFX News Limited*. Shanghai.

Agence France Presse. 2003, April 20. "GM's Output in China Soars as Carmakers Set Up for Shanghai Auto Show." LexisNexis.

Ali, S., Hao Na, David Law, and Paul Buszard. 2005. "World Trade Organisation (WTO) and the Response of Vehicle Manufacturers in China: A Comparative Case Study." *International Journal of Management Practice* 1(1): 57–73.

Alliance of Automobile Manufacturers. 2003. "Economic Facts." http://www.autoalliance.org/ecofacts.htm.

Amsden, A. 1989. *Asia's Next Giant: South Korea and Late Industrialization*. New York: Oxford University Press.

Amsden, A. 2001. *The Rise of "The Rest": Challenges to the West from Late-Industrializing Economies*. New York: Oxford University Press.

An, F., and A. Sauer. 2004. *Comparison of Passenger Vehicle Fuel Economy and Greenhouse Gas Emission Standards around the World*. Washington, DC: Pew Center on Global Change.

An, F., Wu Wei, Jin Yuefu, and He Dongquan. 2003. *Development of China's Light Duty Fuel Consumption Standards*. Conference on Transforming Transportation: New Visions for Urban Transport in China. Washington, DC: World Resources Institute.

Arrow, K. J. 1962. "The Economic Implications of Learning by Doing." *Review of Economic Studies* 29(3): 155–173.

Arrow, K. J. 1969. "Classificatory Notes on the Production and Transmission of Technological Knowledge." *American Economic Review* 59(2): 29–35.

Asia Pulse. 2001, July 10. "China Releases 5 Year Development Plan for Automotive Industry." *Asia Pulse Pte Limited*. LexisNexis.

Asia Pulse. 2002, June 14. "Ford Motor Expects More Car Exports to China." LexisNexis.

Asia Pulse. 2004, December 7. "Beijing Jeep JV Renamed Beijing-Benz-DaimlerChrysler." LexisNexis.

Asia Pulse. 2005, February 4. "China's New Rules on Auto Imports on Sound Footing." LexisNexis.

Auto Asia. 2002, June 5. "Ford Will Build Fiesta-Based Passenger Car in China." LexisNexis.

Avery, N. 2002. "Ford Aims to Start China Joint Venture Production Ahead of Schedule." LexisNexis.

Banks, F. E. 1980. "Oil and the U.S. Dollar." *Energy Economics* 2(3): 142–144.

Baranson, J., and R. Roark. 1985. "Trends in North-South Transfer of High Technology." In N. Rosenberg and C. Frischtak, eds., *International Technology Transfer: Concepts, Measures, and Comparisons*, 24–40. New York: Praeger.

Barber, L. 1994, January 12. "Clinton Places Environment On Top in GATT." LexisNexis.

Beardon, D. 1999. "EPA's Tier 2 Proposal for Stricter Emission Standards: A Fact Sheet." CRS Report to Congress. Washington, DC: Congressional Research Service.

Bloomberg News. 1997, June 11, 2002. "SAIC and GM Sign Contracts to Form New Automotive Company in China." *New York Times* 2003: 4.

Bohi, D. R., and W. D. Montgomery. 1982. *Oil Prices, Energy Security, and Import Policy*. Washington, DC: Resources for the Future.

Bowditch, E. C. 1998. *Opening to the Outside World: The Political Economy of Trade and Foreign Direct Investment in the People's Republic of China*. Los Angeles: University of California.

BP. 2004. "BP Statistical Review of World Energy." www.bp.com/downloads.do?categoryId=9003093&contentId=7005944#1

Bradsher, K. 2003, January 20. "In a Slow Start, Ford Opens an Auto Factory in China." *New York Times* (Chongqing): 2.

Bremer, B., and K. Kerwin, K. K. 2005, May 26. "Here Come Chinese Cars." *Business Week: Online*. www.businessweekonline.

Brooks, H. 1995. "What We Know and Do Not Know about Technology Transfer." *Marshalling Technology for Development*, 83–96. N.R.C. Technology and Development Steering Committee. Washington, DC: National Academy Press.

Burns, L. D., J. B. McCormick, and C. Borroni-Bird. 2002, October. "Vehicle of Change." *Scientific American*: 64–73.

Business Daily Update. 2003. "GM to Roll Out More New Models in China." LexisNexis.

Business Line. 2002, August 8. "Ford India Begins Exporting Auto Parts to Plant in China." LexisNexis.

CATARC. 2000. *Automotive Industry of China 2000*. Tianjin: China Automotive Technology and Research Center (CATARC) and China Association of Automobile Manufacturers.

CATARC. 2001. "The Impact of Foreign Direct Investment on Chinese Auto Industry." *China Auto*. Tianjin: China Automotive Technology and Research Center (CATARC) and China Association of Automobile Manufacturers.

CATARC. 2002a. *Automotive Industry of China 2002*. Tianjin: China Automotive Technology and Research Center (CATARC) and China Association of Automobile Manufacturers.

CATARC. 2002b. "Who Are the Slower Fish among China's Auto Joint Ventures?" *China Auto* 12: 26. Tianjin: China Automotive Technology and Research Center (CATARC) and China Association of Automobile Manufacturers.

CATARC. 2003. "Statistics." *China Auto* 13: 20. Tianjin: China Automotive Technology and Research Center (CATARC) and China Association of Automobile Manufacturers.

CATARC. 2004a. *Automotive Industry of China 2004*. Tianjin: China Automotive Technology and Research Center (CATARC) and China Association of Automobile Manufacturers.

CATARC. 2004b. "Reprint of the Auto Industry Development Policy." *China Auto* 14(5).

CATARC. 2005. "Auto Production and Sales." *China Auto* 15(1).

Chan, C. C. 2002. "The State of the Art of Electric and Hybrid Vehicles." *Proceedings of the IEEE* 90(2): 247–275.

Chang'An Automobile Group. 2002. *Chang'An Automobile (Group) Liability Co., Ltd. Company Report*. Chongqing: Chang'An Automobile Group.

China Business Information Network. 1998a, November 9. "China: GM Confident of China Market." LexisNexis.

China Business Information Network. 1998b, September 25. "China-Vehicle Emission Policies to Force Polluters Off Roads." LexisNexis.

China Daily. 2004, December 18. "GM Charges Chery for Alleged Mini Car Piracy." *China Daily*.

ChinaOnline. 2001, December 21. "China-First Ford-Chang'An Sedan to Debut in March." LexisNexis.

ChinaOnline. 2002, March 28. "China—Ford Calls on China to Allow Majority Stakes in JVs." LexisNexis.

China Post. 2002, January 24. "Ford Inaugurates New Design and Research Center in Taiwan." LexisNexis.

"China's Car Industry: Ich Bin Ein Beijinger." 1995, July 15. *The Economist* 336: 47.

Christenson, C. D. 1997. "Fuel Cell System Technologies and Application Issues." *Energy Engineering* 94(2): 36–46.

Chuan, Q. 2004, November 17. "US Technology Helps Reduce Car Emissions." *China Daily.* Beijing.

Chudnovsky, D., and A. Lopez. 2002. "Globalization, Foreign Direct Investment, and Sustainable Human Development." In K. P. Gallagher and J. Werksman, eds., *The Earthscan Reader on International Trade and Sustainable Development,* 45–76. London: Earthscan.

CIIC (China Internet Information Center). 2002. "China's Leading Car Producer Sets Up R&D Center." LexisNexis.

Conte, M., A. Iacobazzi, M. Ronchetti, and R. Vellone. 2001. "Hydrogen Economy for a Sustainable Development: State-of-the-Art and Technological Perspectives." *Journal of Power Sources* 100: 171–187.

Dahlman, C., B. Ross-Larson, and L. Westphal. 1987. "Managing Technological Development: Lessons from Newly Industrializing Countries." *World Development* 15(6): 759–775.

DaimlerChrysler. 2002. "Beijing Jeep." http://www.daimlerchrysler.com/company/worldwide/facts/beijing_e.htm.

Davis, S. C., and S. W. Diegel. 2002. *Transportation Energy Databook.* Washington, DC: Oak Ridge National Laboratory, Center for Transportation Analysis, U.S. Department of Energy.

de Meyer, A. 2001. "Technology Transfer into China: Preparing for a New Era." *European Management Journal* 19(2): 140–144.

Dow Jones International News. 2001. "China OK's Chongqing Changan Ford Compact Car Venture." LexisNexis.

"Dream Machine." 2005, June 4. *The Economist* 24–26.

EC. 2001. "Emission Standards for Road Vehicles." *EU Energy and Transport Figures.* European Commission. http://europa.eu.int/energy_transport/etif/environment/emissions_cars.html.

Economist Intelligence Unit. 2005. *Country Profile: China.* London: Economist Intelligence Unit Ltd.

Economy, E. 1999. "Painting China Green." *Foreign Affairs* 78(2): 14–18.

Economy, E. 2004. *The River Runs Black: The Environmental Challenge to China's Future.* Ithaca, NY: Cornell University Press.

EIA. 2001. "China: Environmental Issues." *Country Briefs.* Washington, DC: Energy Information Administration (EIA), U.S. Department of Energy.

EIA. 2002. *China Country Analysis Brief.* Washington, DC: Energy Information Administration (EIA), U.S. Department of Energy.

EIU DataServices. 2003. "EIU Country Data." Bureau van Dijk and Economist Intelligence Unit.

Fackler, M. 2002, December 21. "GM Adds Fourth Factory in China, Upping Production Despite Competition." LexisNexis.

Fairbank, J. K. 1951. *The United States and China*. Cambridge, MA: Harvard University Press.

Faison, S. 1998, December 18. GM Opens Buick Plant in Shanghai. *New York Times*: 1.

FBIS (Foreign Broadcasting Information Service). 1994, July 4. "Commentator Urges Boosting Auto Industry Growth."

FBIS (Foreign Broadcasting Information Service). 1995, November 14. "Weaponry Industry Turns to Auto-Making."

Fisher, R. 1995. "Negotiating Power: Getting and Using Influence." In J. W. Breslin and J. Rubin, eds., *Negotiation Theory and Practice*, 127–140. Cambridge, MA: Program on Negotiation, Harvard Law School.

Fisher-Vanden, K. 2003. "Management Structure and Technology Diffusion in Chinese State-Owned Enterprises." *Energy Policy* 31: 247–257.

Ford. 2002. *Ford Motor Company Brochure*. Beijing: Ford Motor (China) Ltd.

Freeman, C. 1992. *The Economics of Hope*. London: Pinter.

French, H. F. 1998. *Investing in the Future: Harnessing Private Capital Flows for Environmentally Sustainable Development*. Washington, DC: Worldwatch Institute.

Fu, L., J. Hao, D. He, K. He, and P. Li. 2001. "Assessment of Vehicular Pollution in China." *Journal of the Air and Waste Management Association* 51(5): 658–668.

Gallagher, K. P. 2004. *Free Trade and the Environment: Mexico, NAFTA, and Beyond*. Stanford, CA: Stanford University Press.

GAO. 2000. *Cooperative Research: Results of U.S.-Industry Partnership to Develop a New Generation of Vehicles*. Washington, DC: U.S. General Accounting Office.

GEF. 2001. *Project Brief: Demonstration for Fuel Cell Bus Commercialization*. Washington, DC: Global Environment Facility.

GM. 2001. "General Motors—Company, Corporate Information, General Motors China Group." www.gm.com/company/corp_info/global_locations/china.html.

Goldemberg, J. 1998. "Leapfrog Energy Technologies." *Energy Policy* 2(10): 729–741.

Gong, Z. 2001, April 26. "Ford Gets Its China JV." *China Daily* (New York): 5.

Gong, Z. 2003, March 11. "Ford Refutes Criticism of Fiesta." *China Daily* (New York). www.chinadaily.com/en/doc/2003-03/04/content_157539.htm

Graham, M. 2000. "Paddy Fields to Full Production." *Industry Week* 249: 54–60.

Griliches, Z. 1996. "The Discovery of the Residual: A Historical Note." *Journal of Economic Literature* 34(3): 1324–1330.

Grossman, G. M., and A. B. Kruger. 1991. *Environmental Impacts of a North American Free Trade Agreement.* Cambridge, MA: National Bureau of Economic Research.

Grubler, A. 1998. *Technology and Global Change.* Cambridge: Cambridge University Press.

Guerin, T. F. 2001. "Transferring Environmental Technologies to China: Recent Developments and Constraints." *Technological Forecasting and Social Change* 67: 55–75.

Halberstam, D. 1986. *The Reckoning.* New York: Avon Books.

Harwit, E. 1995. *China's Automobile Industry: Policies, Problems, and Prospects.* New York: M. E. Sharpe.

He, D., and M. Wang. 2001, January 7–11. "China Vehicle Growth in the Next 30 Years: Consequences on Motor Fuel Demand and CO_2 Emissions." *Annual Meeting of Transportation Research Board.* http://www.transportation. anl.gov/pdfs/TA/124.pdf.

Holdren, J. P., G. Daily, and P. Ehrlich. 1995. "The Meaning of Sustainability: Biogeophysical Aspects." In M. Munasinghe and W. Shearer, eds., *Defining and Measuring Sustainability: The Biogeophysical Foundation,* 3–17. Washington, DC: United Nations University and The World Bank.

Hu, A. G. 1999. *Institutions, Organizations, and Technological Innovation in Chinese Industry.* PhD diss. Department of International Economics and Finance. Boston: Brandeis University.

Huang, Y. 2002. *Analysis on Rules and Trends of the Revision of Chinese Industrial Policies Related to Auto Industry.* Joint Workshop on Clean Vehicle Development and Deployment, Beijing, Harvard University, China Ministry of Science and Technology, and China Automotive Technology and Research Center.

Hymer, S. 1976. *The International Operations of National Firms: A Study of Direct Foreign Investment.* Cambridge, MA: MIT Press.

Hyundai Motor Corporation. 2002. "Corporate Information." http://www. hyundai-motor.com/eng/intro/index.html.

Ibison, D., and R. McGregor. 2002, June 12. "China Exports First Cars to US." *Financial Times* (London): 7.

IISD and WWF. 2001. *Private Rights, Public Problems: A Guide to NAFTA's Controversial Chapter on Investor Rights.* Canada: International Institute for Sustainable Development.

Ingrassia, P., and J. B. White. 1994. *Comeback: The Fall and Rise of the American Automobile Industry.* New York: Simon & Schuster.

ITA. 2003a. "Industry Fact Sheets: Autos and Auto Parts." http://www.mac.doc. gov/China/Docs/industryfactsheets/autos.html.

ITA. 2003b. "Top 50 Partners in Total U.S. Trade in 2001." www.ita.doc.gov/td/ industry/otea/usfth/aggregate/H01T09.html.

Jahiel, A. 1998. "The Organization of Environmental Protection in China." *China Quarterly* 156: 757–787.

Jiang, Z. 1999. Speech at the Opening Ceremony. High-Level Segment of the 5th Meeting of the Conference of Parties to the Vienna Convention and the 11th Meeting of the Parties to the Montreal Protocol, Beijing.

Jorgenson, D. W. 1982. "Energy Prices and Productivity Growth." In L. Matthiessen, ed., *The Impact of Rising Oil Prices on the World Economy*, 25–39. London: Macmillan Press.

Kim, L., and C. Dahlman. 1992. "Technology Policy for Industrialization: An Integrative Framework and Korea's Experience." *Research Policy* 21: 437–452.

Kim, L., and R. R. Nelson. 2000. *Technology, Learning, and Innovation: Experiences of Newly Industrializing Economies*. Cambridge: Cambridge University Press.

Kline, S. J., and N. Rosenberg. 1986. "An Overview of Innovation." In R. Landau and N. Rosenberg, eds., *The Positive Sum Strategy: Harnessing Technology for Economic Growth*. Washington, DC: National Academy Press.

Kobos, P. H., J. D. Erickson, and T. Drennen. 2003. "Scenario Analysis of Chinese Passenger Vehicle Growth." *Contemporary Economic Policy* 21(2): 200–217.

Kraar, L. 1999. "China's Car Guy." *Fortune* 140: 238–246.

Kranzberg, M. 1986. "The Technical Elements in International Technology Transfer: Historical Perspectives." In J. R. McIntyre and D. S. Papp, eds., *The Political Economy of International Technology Transfer*. Westport, CT: Greenwood Press.

Kurtenbach, E. 2005, June 2. "Small Carmakers Rise in China's Large Market." *Associated Press* (Shanghai).

Kyodo News Service. 2002, July 18. "Mazda Launches Small Passenger Car in China." LexisNexis.

Lall, S. 2000. "Technological Change and Industrialization in the Asian Newly Industrializing Economies: Achievements and Challenges." In L. Kim and R. R. Nelson, eds., *Technology, Learning, and Innovation*. Cambridge: Cambridge University Press.

Lanjouw, J. O., and A. Mody. 1996. "Innovation and the International Diffusion of Environmentally Responsive Technology." *Research Policy* 25: 549–571.

LBNL. 2001. *China Energy Databook v. 5.0*. Berkeley, CA: Lawrence Berkeley National Laboratory (LBNL) and Energy Research Institute.

Lee, K., and C. Lim. 2001. "Technological Regimes, Catching-Up and Leapfrogging: Findings from the Korean Industries." *Research Policy* 20: 459–483.

Leicester, J. 2000, October 24. "General Motors Targets China's Middle Class with New Compact Car." LexisNexis.

Li, S., and Z. Wang. 1998. *The Global and Domestic Impact of China Joining the World Trade Organization.* Washington, DC: Development Research Center of the China State Council, Project of China Economic Research Program, Washington Center for China Studies, Ford Foundation.

Lienert, I. 1982. "The Macroeconomic Effects of the 1979/1980 Oil Price Rise on Four Nordic Countries." In L. Matthiessen, ed., *The Impact of Rising Oil Prices on the World Economy*, 61–79. London: Macmillan Press.

Liu, M. 2002, April 29. "Road Warriors; Middle-Class Chinese Are Going Car Crazy, Buying Autos and Hitting the Road as Never Before." *Newsweek* 26.

"Losses at Venture in China." 1998, July 14. *New York Times* 2.

Ma, X., and L. Ortolano. 2000. *Environmental Regulation in China: Institutions, Enforcement, and Compliance.* Oxford: Rowman & Littlefield.

Mann, J. 1989. *Beijing Jeep.* New York: Simon & Schuster.

Markus, F. 2003. "China Plans $10 bn Oil Reserve." http://news.bbc.co.uk/2/hi/business/2814825.stm.

Martinot, E., J. E. Sinton, and B. M. Haddad. 1997. "International Technology Transfer for Climate Change Mitigation and the Cases of Russia and China." *Annual Review of Energy and Environment* 22: 357–401.

McDonald, A., and L. Schrattenholzer. 2001. "Learning Rates for Energy Technologies." *Energy Policy* 29: 255–261.

McGregor, R. 2002, August 21. "VW Loses Chinese Lead but Is Still in the Race." LexisNexis Academic Universe.

METI. 2005. "Report on the WTO Inconsistency of Trade Policies by Major Trading Partners." www.meti.go.jp/english/report/data/gCT05_1coe.html.

Metz, B., O. R. Davidson, J. W. Martens, S. N. van Rooijen, and L. Van Wie McGrory, eds. 2000. *Methodological and Technological Issues in Technology Transfer.* New York: Cambridge University Press.

Mitsubishi Motors Corporation. 2002. *Facts & Figures.* Tokyo: Mitsubishi Motors Corporation.

Moriera, J. R., and J. Goldemberg. 1999. "The Alcohol Program." *Energy Policy* 27: 229–245.

Murphy, J. 2001. "Making the Energy Transition in Rural East Africa: Is Leapfrogging An Alternative?" *Technological Forecasting and Social Change* 68: 173–193.

NBS. 2002. *The Car Output in November Has Exceeded 110,000.* Beijing: National Bureau of Statistics of China.

Needham, J. 1969. *The Grand Titration: Science and Society in East and West.* London: Allen & Unwin.

North, D. C. 1965. "Industrialization in the United States." In H. J. Habakkuk and M. Postan, ed., *The Cambridge Economic History of Europe*, vol. 6, 673–705. Cambridge: Cambridge University Press.

NRC. 2000. *Research Program of the Partnership for a New Generation of Vehicles: Sixth Report.* Washington, DC: National Research Council.

OECD. 2000. *The OECD Guidelines for Multinational Enterprises.* www.oecd.org/dataoecd/56/36/1922428.pdf.

OECD. 2002. *Foreign Direct Investment for Development: Maximizing Benefits, Minimizing Costs.* Paris: Organization for Economic Cooperation and Development.

OECD. 2003. "Policy Brief: The OECD Guidelines for Multinational Enterprises." http://www.oecd.org/EN/document/0,EN-document-93-3-no-14-4404-0,00.html.

Ohshita, S. B., and L. Ortolano. 2002. "The Promise and Pitfalls of Japanese Cleaner Coal Technology Transfer to China." *International Journal of Technology Transfer and Commercialization* 1(1–2): 56–81.

Pan, J., Huaiguo Hu, Fei Yu, and Limin Cheng. 2004. "Automobiles." In R. Ye and D. Runnals, ed., *An Environmental Impact Assessment of China's WTO Accession*, 107–135. Winnipeg, Manitoba: International Institute for Sustainable Development.

People's Daily. 2003, January 14. "China Waits for Right Time for Fuel Tax Launch." *People's Daily* (Beijing).

People's Daily. 2005, March 7. "Auto Parts Imports Face Higher Tariffs." *People's Daily* (Beijing).

Perry, J. C. 1994. *Facing West: Americans and the Opening of the Pacific.* Westport, CT: Praeger.

Ramakrishnan, N. 2002, June 24. "Ford China Teams Get Hands-on at Chennai Unit." LexisNexis.

Rawski, T. G. 1989. *Economic Growth in Pre-War China.* Berkeley: University of California Press.

Reddy, A. C. 1996. *A Macro Perspective on Technology Transfer.* Westport, CT: Quorum Books.

Reddy, M. N., and L. M. Zhao. 1990. "International Technology Transfer: A Review." *Research Policy* 19(4): 285–307.

Rodrik, D. 2001, October. "The Global Governance of Trade: As If Development Really Mattered." http://www.undp.org/mainundp/propoor/docs/pov_globalgovernancetrade_pub.pdf.

Rogers, E. M. 1995. *Diffusion of Innovations.* New York: Free Press.

Rosenberg, N., and C. Frischtak. 1985. *International Technology Transfer: Concepts, Measures, and Comparisons.* New York: Praeger.

Saggi, K. 2002. "Trade, Foreign Direct Investment, and International Technology Transfer: A Survey." *World Bank Research Observer* 17(2): 191–235.

SAIC. 2003. "Company Website." http://www.saicgroup.com/saic01/fore/english/company/jituan/jituan_default.htm.

Salacuse, J. W. 1999. "How Should the Lamb Negotiate with the Lion? Power in International Negotiations." In D. Kolb, ed., *Negotiation Eclectics: Essays in Memory of Jeffrey Z. Rubin*, 87–99. Cambridge, MA: PON Books.

Salvatore, D. 1993. *International Economics*. New York: Macmillan.

Schmidheiny, S. 1992. *Changing Course: A Global Business Perspective on Development and the Environment*. Cambridge, MA: MIT Press.

Schnepp, O., M. A. von Glinow, and A. Bhambri. 1990. *United States–China Technology Transfer*. Englewood Cliffs, NJ: Prentice Hall.

Schumpeter, J. A. 1934. *The Theory of Economic Development: An Inquiry into Profits, Capital, Credit, Interest, and the Business Cycle*. Trans. R. Opie. Cambridge, MA: Harvard University Press.

Shao, M., and Y. Zhang. 2001. *Current Air Quality Problem and Control Strategies for Vehicular Emissions in China*. Beijing: Center for Environmental Sciences, Peking University.

Shapiro, J. 2001. *Mao's War against Nature: Politics and the Environment in Revolutionary China*. New York: Cambridge University Press.

Sharif, N. M. 1989. "Technological Leapfrogging: Implications for Developing Countries." *Technological Forecasting and Social Change* 36: 201–208.

SinoCast. 2003. "Beijing Jeep Accredits Turning Loss into Profit to Staff Cutting." LexisNexis.

SinoCast. 2005, June 4. "GM to Launch New Car Models in 2005." LexisNexis Academic Universe.

Smith, J. F., Jr. 1997. *GM's Thinking on China*. Saint Louis, MO: Washington University.

Solow, R. M. 1957. "Technical Change and the Aggregate Production Function." *Review of Economics and Statistics* 39(3): 312–320.

Sperling, D., Zhenlong Lin, and Peter Hamilton. 2004. *Chinese Rural Vehicles: An Exploratory Analysis of Technology, Economics, Industrial Organization, Energy Use, and Policy*. Davis: Institute of Transporation Studies, University of California.

Standard & Poor's Register of Corporations. 2005a. "DaimlerChrysler AG." LexisNexis Academic Universe.

Standard & Poor's Register of Corporations. 2005b. "Ford Motor Company." LexisNexis.

Standard & Poor's Register of Corporations. 2005c. "General Motors Corp." LexisNexis.

State Economic and Trade Commission of China. 2001. "Tenth Five-Year Plan (2001–2005) for the Development of the Automotive Industry." Beijing: Asia Pulse.

Stern, D. 2002. "Progress on the Environmental Kuznets Curve?" In K. P. Gallagher and J. Werksman, eds., *The Earthscan Reader on International Trade and Sustainable Development*, 91–114. London: Earthscan Publications.

Stiglitz, J. 1989. "Markets, Market Failures, and Development." *American Economic Review* 72(2): 196–203.

Trade Development Council. 2005. *China Removes Car Import Quotas by 2005*. Hong Kong: Hong Kong Trade Development Council.

Treece, J. B. 2002a. "DCX Moves to Jump-Start China Jeep Venture." *Automotive News* 76: 3.

Treece, J. B. 2002b. "Industry Recatches 'China Fever.'" *Automotive News* 37.

Trindade, S. C., T. Siddiqi, and E. Martinot. 2000. "Managing Technological Change in Support of the Climate Change Convention: A Framework for Decison-making." In B. D. Metz, R. Ogunlade, Jan-Willem Martens, Sascha N. M. van Rooijen, and Laura Van Wie McGrory, *Methodological and Technological Issues in Technology Transfer*, 49–62. New York: Cambridge University Press.

Tuan, Y.-F. 1973. "Ambiguity in Attitudes toward Environment." *Annals of the Association of American Geographers* 63(4): 411–423.

UNCTAD. 2002. *World Investment Report*. New York: United Nations Conference on Trade and Development (UNCTAD).

Unruh, G. C. 2000. "Understanding Carbon Lock-In." *Energy Policy* 28: 817–830.

U.S. Embassy Beijing. 2000, December. "The Cost of Environmental Degradation in China." http://www.usembassy-china.org.cn/sandt/CostofPollution-web.html.

Van Vorst, W. M. D., and R. S. George. 1997. "Impact of the California Clean Air Act." *International Journal of Hydrogen Energy* 22(1): 31–38.

Waley, A., Trans. 1989. *Analects of Confucius*. New York: Vintage Books.

Walsh, M. P. 2000. "Transportation and the Environment in China." *China Environment Series*, no. 3.

Walsh, M. P. 2003. "Clean Fuels in China." *Sinosphere* 6(1): 17–20.

Warhurst, A. 1991. "Technology Transfer and the Development of China's Offshore Oil Industry." *World Development* 19(8): 1055–1073.

Watson, R. T. C., ed. 2001. *Third Assessment Report*. London: Oxford University Press.

WHO. 2004. *Environmental Health Country Profile: China*. Geneva: World Health Organization (WHO).

World Bank. 1997. *Clear Water, Blue Skies*. Washington, DC: World Bank.

World Bank. 2000. *World Development Report: Attacking Poverty*. New York: Oxford University Press.

World Bank. 2002. *World Development Indicators*, 18–20. Washington, DC: World Bank.

World Bank. 2005a. "Overview: International Comparison Program." http:web.worldbank.org.

World Bank. 2005b. *World Development Indicators Database.* Washington, DC: World Bank. www.worldbank.org/data/countrydata.html.

WTO. 2003a. "The Organization: Membership, Alliances, and Bureaucracy." www.wto.org/english/thewto_e/whatis_e/tif_e/org3.thm.

WTO. 2003b. "TRIMS: Background." www.wto.org/english/thewto_e/whatis_e/eol/e/wto05/wto5_3.htm.

Wu, F. 2002. "New Partners or Old Brothers: GONGOs in Transnational Advocacy in China." *China Environment Series*(5): 45–58.

Xinhua. 1999. "About 208 Million Chinese Rise from Poverty in Past 20 Years." *Xinhua News Agency.*

Xinhua. 2002a, May 17. "Beijingers Concerned about Environment: Survey Shows." LexisNexis.

Xinhua. 2002b, August 5. "China's Leading Car Producer Sets up R&D Center." LexisNexis.

Xinhua. 2002c, May 31. "Chinese Children Have 28 Anxieties: Survey." LexisNexis.

Xinhua Economic News Service. 2002, September 5. "Output and Sales of Motor Vehicles in First Half." LexisNexis.

Xinhua Economic News Service. 2005a, June 3. "2005 Investment Plans of Multinationals in China." LexisNexis.

Xinhua Economic News Service. 2005b. "China's Auto Market Sees Rebound from Price War to Technology Competition." LexisNexis.

Xinhua Economic News Service. 2005c, June 3. "New Auto Rules State Joint Venture Guidelines." LexisNexis.

Xinhua Financial Network News. 2005a, January 5. "China's Changan Auto 2004 Revenue Climbs 35.32% to 28.25 Billion Yuan." LexisNexis.

Xinhua Financial Network News. 2005b, February 7. "Shanghai Auto 2004 Net Profit Up 30.41% Despite Industry's Slower Growth." LexisNexis.

Xinhua Financial Network News. 2005c, January 31. "Shanghai VW, FAW-VW, Shanghai GM Dominate China Sedan Sales in 2004." LexisNexis.

Xu, B. 2000. "Multinational Enterprises, Technology Diffusion, and Host Country Productivity." *Journal of Development Economics* 62: 477–493.

Xu, B. 2002. *Arrangement on "Auto Fuel Economy Standards and Fuel Efficiency Promotion Policies of China."* Workshop on Cleaner Vehicles in the U.S. and China, Beijing, Harvard University, China Ministry of Science and Technololgy, and China Automotive Technology and Research Center (CATARC).

Xu, X. 2000. "China and the Middle East: Cross-Investment in the Energy Sector." *Middle East Policy,* 7(3): 122–136.

Yin, J. Z. 1992. "Technological Capabilities as Determinants of the Success of Technology Transfer Projects." *Technological Forecasting and Social Change* (42): 17–29.

Zarsky, L. 1999a. *Havens, Halos, and Spaghetti: Untangling the Evidence about Foreign Direct Investment and the Environment.* The Hague: Organization for Economic Cooperation and Development.

Zarsky, L. 1999b. "International Investment Rules and the Environment: Stuck in the Mud?" *Foreign Policy in Focus* 4(22): 1–3.

Zhang, J. 2002. *Review and Prospect of China Auto Industry.* Joint Workshop on Clean Vehicle Development and Deployment, Harvard University, China Ministry of Science and Technology, and China Automotive Technology and Research Center (CATARC).

Zhao, J. 2002. *Moving to Cleaner Vehicles: Alternative Fuel Vehicle Programs in the United States and China.* Joint Workshop on Cleaner Vehicles in the U.S. and China, Beijing, Harvard University, China Ministry of Science and Technology, and China Automotive Technology and Research Center (CATARC).

Zoia, D. 2001. "Ready to Blossom." *Ward's Auto World.* 37: 37–39.

Index

Urban and Industrial Environments

Series editor: Robert Gottlieb, Henry R. Luce Professor of Urban and Environmental Policy, Occidental College

The U.S. Paper Industry and Sustainable Production: An Argument for Restructuring
Maureen Smith

Human Settlements and Planning for Ecological Sustainability: The Case of Mexico City
Keith Pezzoli

Greening the Ivory Tower: Improving the Environmental Track Record of Universities, Colleges, and Other Institutions
Sarah Hammond Creighton

Making Microchips: Policy, Globalization, and Economic Restructuring in the Semiconductor Industry
Jan Mazurek

The Land That Could Be: Environmentalism and Democracy in the Twenty-First Century
William A. Shutkin

Reclaiming the Environmental Debate: The Politics of Health in a Toxic Culture
Richard Hofrichter, ed.

Environmentalism Unbound: Exploring New Pathways for Change
Robert Gottlieb

Materials Matter: Toward a Sustainable Materials Policy
Kenneth Geiser

Silent Spill: The Organization of an Industrial Crisis
Thomas D. Beamish

Concrete and Clay: Reworking Nature in New York City
Matthew Gandy

Garbage Wars: The Struggle for Environmental Justice in Chicago
David Naguib Pellow

Just Sustainabilities: Development in an Unequal World
Julian Agyeman, Robert D. Bullard, and Bob Evans, eds.

Uneasy Alchemy: Citizens and Experts in Louisiana's Chemical Corridor Disputes
Barbara L. Allen

Community-Driven Regulation: Balancing Development and the Environment in Vietnam
Dara O'Rourke

Labor and the Environmental Movement: The Quest for Common Ground
Brian K. Obach

Sustainability on Campus: Stories and Strategies for Change
Peggy F. Barlett and Geoffrey W. Chase, eds.

Diamond: A Struggle for Environmental Justice in Louisiana's Chemical Corridor
Steve Lerner

Street Science: Community Knowledge and Environmental Health Justice
Jason Corburn

Urban Place: Reconnecting with the Natural World
Peggy F. Barlett, ed.

Power, Justice, and the Environment: A Critical Appraisal of the Environmental Justice Movement
David Naguib Pellow and Robert J. Brulle, eds.

The Code of the City: Standards and the Hidden Language of Place Making
Eran Ben-Joseph

Precautionary Tools for Reshaping Environmental Policy
Nancy J. Myers and Carolyn Raffensperger, eds.

China Shifts Gears: Automakers, Oil, Pollution, and Development
Kelly Sims Gallagher